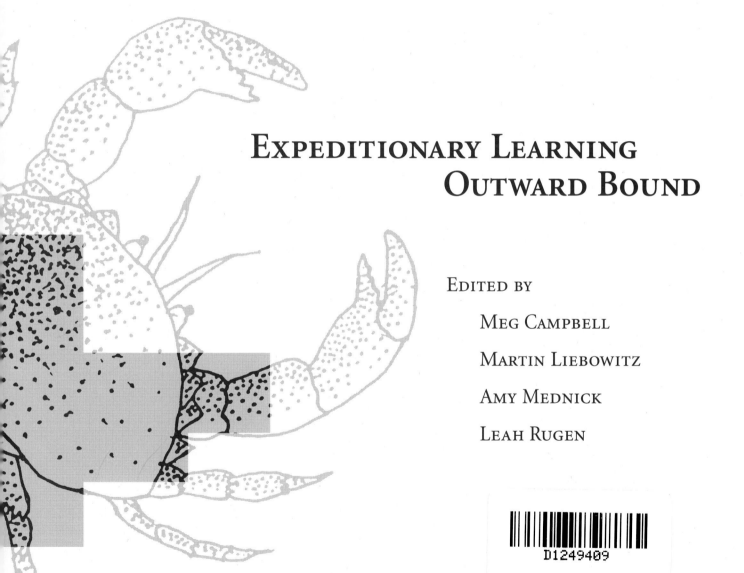

GUIDE FOR PLANNING A LEARNING EXPEDITION

EXPEDITIONARY LEARNING OUTWARD BOUND

EDITED BY

MEG CAMPBELL

MARTIN LIEBOWITZ

AMY MEDNICK

LEAH RUGEN

D1249409

KENDALL/HUNT PUBLISHING COMPANY
4050 Westmark Drive   Dubuque, Iowa 52002

Guide For Planning a Learning Expedition

CONTENTS

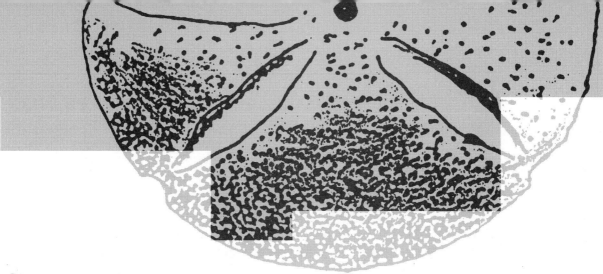

Acknowledgments

We would like to thank the many teachers, administrators, students, and families whose work informs every aspect of the guide. It is impossible to name them all. Particular thanks go to the following educators who contributed to drafts or provided the examples that illustrate the guide:

Kim Archung, Joel Barsky, Dolores Bentham, Ron Berger, Eloise Biscoe, Rebecca Bordelon, Loretta Brady, Angela Budde, Blanca Burgos, Paul Clifford, Christine Cziko, Tammy Duehr, Phil Dyer, Renee Ehle, Shari Flatt, Laura Flaxman, Deb Fordice, Bill Fulton, Nora Gill, Phil Gonring, Kathy Greeley, Christine Griffin, Scott Hartl, James Hunt, Sarah Johnson, Angela Jolliffe, Edi Juricic, Brian LaFerriere, Steven Levy, Mary Lynn Lewark, Betty Lunt, Jonathan Mann, Angela Mattison, Javier Mendez, Susan McCray, Karen MacDonald, Betsey McGee, Wanda Muriel, Roberto Porrata-Doria, Connie Russell-Rodriguez, Cheryl Sims, Leo Snow, Hector Soto, Elaine Stanton, Vivian Stephens, Candy Systra, Denis Udall, Elida Vazquez-Bera, Kim Verreault, and Mark Weiss.

We especially thank the following students whose artwork illustrates the guide: Matt Birch, Jessica Bowers, Joey Burns, Eric Christ, Mimi Durrah, Brett Farran, James Flynn, Tiffiny Green, Christina Hinkel, Gene Ninneman, John Ogelsby, Melissa Ruh, and Jeremy Vasquez of Central Alternative High

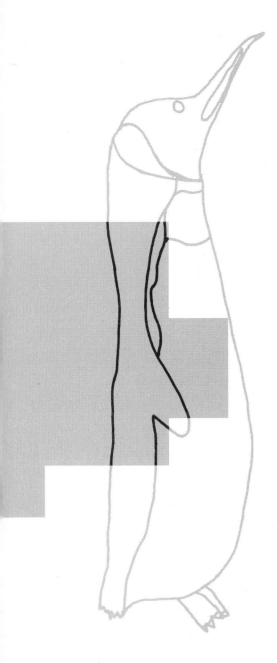

School in Dubuque, Iowa; John Earle, William Huggins, Casey C. Paulozzi, Stephen Taylor, and Kevin Williams of Clairemont Elementary School in Decatur, Ga.; Isaiah Abreo, Josh Feehan, Ashley Gottschalk of Fulton Intermediate School in Dubuque, Iowa; Richard Torres of Harbor School in Boston, Mass.; Alex Adrian, Chang Ho, Aaron Huntley, Srecko Maric, Cecily Merrill, Liz Mowatt, Jimmy Nguyen, Thao Nguyen, Isaiah Oliver, Alex Pringle, and Lindsay Rowe of King Middle School in Portland, Maine; Amethyst Barron and Mark Skinner of Lincoln School in Dubuque, Iowa; Maegan Hudson of Macon Elementary School in Memphis, Tenn.; Stephen Haynes of Peoples Middle School in Cincinnati, Ohio; Roberto Aponte, Karen Barnes, Marquia Lawson, and Carlos Santiago of Rafael Hernandez School in Boston, Mass.; Brett Beadle, Anya Bishop, Danny Breitbach, Adam Coates, Charles Erickson, Ed Frederick, Kevin Kelchen, Mark Kelly, Chris Konzen, Marty Malone, Chad Pfab, Zachary Pickel, Jacob Tharp, and Ty Welu of Table Mound Elementary School in Dubuque, Iowa.

Portions of this guide were inspired by the Coalition of Essential Schools.

Special thanks to New American Schools for critical support of our work.

Sample web illustration on page 12 by Gail Gardner.

Book cover and interior pages designed by Carroll Conquest, Conquest Design.

INTRODUCTION

The purpose of this guide is to provide help and structure to teachers in planning, reflecting on, and revising learning expeditions. There is no way to capture "curriculum" fully in paper and ink. Learning expeditions really exist in the constant interactions among the teacher, the students, and the focus of learning—topics, questions, experiments, projects, skills, texts, and materials. They are alive and changing every minute. But in order to think, prepare, and collaborate, we need common language and ways of organizing. That is what this guide is intended to provide. The emphasis here is on planning, revising, and documenting curricula rather than on providing detailed illustrations and suggestions for instructional practice.

Of course, curriculum, instruction, and assessment are completely interconnected and reflected in every element of the learning expedition, and a wide range of resources is needed in order to inform the hundreds of instructional decisions a teacher makes every day. This guide is meant to be useful to K–12 teachers, so it is assumed that they will rely on resources specific to developmental stages of learning and to different disciplines. Finally, the framework is meant to be adapted to individual needs. It is *not* meant to present a prescribed or formulaic approach to planning and teaching.

Although the guide is aimed at individual teachers and teams, it is part of a design to help whole schools grow and improve. As the first core practice of the Expeditionary Learning Outward Bound design, learning expeditions are both the entry point for a school implementing the design and the foundation for improving student learning. Learning expeditions are taught, revised, and improved in the context of four other interrelated core practices: Reflection and Critique, School Culture, School Structures, and School Review. Together these five core practices provide a comprehensive framework for school improvement, each core practice building on and supporting the others.

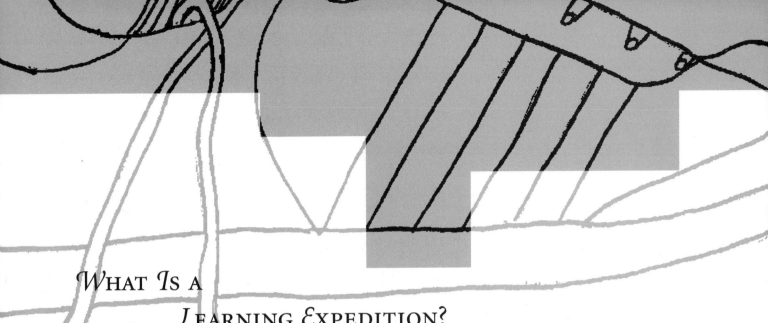

WHAT IS A LEARNING EXPEDITION?

*L*earning expeditions are long-term, in-depth investigations of a topic that engage students in the world through authentic projects, fieldwork, and service. The work students do within learning expeditions centers on critical thinking, essential skills and habits, and character development. Ongoing assessment is woven throughout the expeditions, pushing students to higher levels of performance in pursuit of academic excellence.

Learning expeditions grow out of the metaphor of an Outward Bound wilderness expedition. Although they begin with clear goals and a plan, expeditions take unexpected turns and encounter adventure. They take teachers and students beyond the boundaries of what they already know. Asking people to draw on the resources found within the group, wilderness expeditions and learning expeditions require them to meet challenges, solve problems, and arrive at a destination that at first seemed unattainable. Individuals on an expedition must persevere and exercise judgment. Members of an expedition team develop close relationships and learn to take care of each other well because they are thrown together in facing a challenge, must rely on each other, and live together closely.

Students in the midst of a learning expedition engage with challenging content and skills in a context that has meaning and importance. Each expedition proceeds through distinct stages. In the beginning, students are immersed in an experience that captures their interest in the topic. This immersion is followed by a sequence of skill building and closely supervised project work, and, finally, by a more independent challenge in which students apply and present their learning to an audience. In Outward Bound wilderness expeditions, similar stages are called "Training," "Main," and "Final." Throughout the learning expedition, teachers hold high expectations for all students, and provide the time and structure for the sustained effort needed to achieve high levels of work through multiple revisions. To honor the hard work of everyone involved, an expedition culminates in a celebration that often includes families and community members.

Learning expeditions challenge students to learn the core concepts and thinking approaches of different disciplines, to see issues from multiple perspectives, and to apply the approaches, concepts, and tools of disciplines and professions to solve real-world problems. They encompass all of the learning that occurs around a given topic—reading and discussion, skill building and practice, project work (including drafting and revision), field-work, and so forth. Expeditions are often integrated across disciplines, though they are more likely to focus on a single discipline in secondary school.

In an Expeditionary Learning school, learning expeditions are the central focus of curriculum and instruction, not an add-on or enrichment activity. They are the primary way that students learn the content and skills they need to understand and an important part of the strategy to prepare students for required tests. The topics, questions, and learning goals that give shape to learning expeditions are informed by district and state standards.

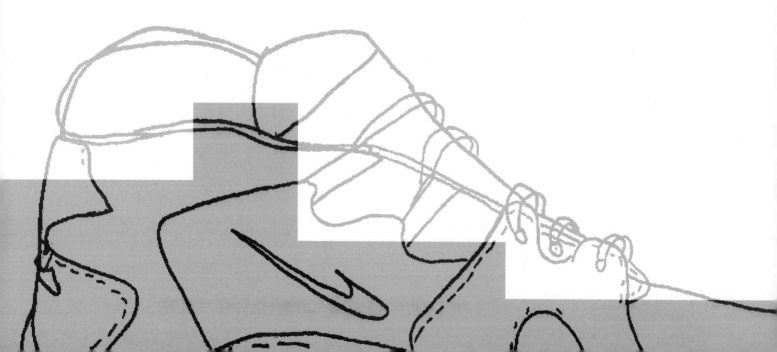

QUALITIES OF LEARNING EXPEDITIONS

Learning expeditions:

~ embody the Expeditionary Learning design principles.

~ build a strong connection to the world, inside and outside the classroom; they focus on linking the classroom and the outside world, fully drawing on school and community resources.

~ have high standards and stakes; there is an emphasis on student work of consequence, quality, and value in major projects as well as ongoing smaller tasks and assignments.

~ focus on assessment and understanding—fostering a continuous process of reflection, critique, and revision among teachers and students. They develop the habit of reflecting on their work and seeking feedback.

~ foster an ethic and practice of service—in the classroom, school, and wider community.

~ ask teachers to draw on their passion for learning and alertness to opportunity, and endeavor to help their students share the same.

~ support students in taking responsibility for their own learning.

~ create a spirit of adventure and challenge that permeates the classroom and school.

~ require change in the use of time and space to make room for in-depth study, fieldwork, collaboration among teachers, and multidisciplinary connections.

~ call for leadership, teamwork, and organization on the part of teachers and students.

~ require new roles for learners; groups of students collaborate as crews, and individual students become explorers, apprentices, and even experts.

PLANNING A

LEARNING EXPEDITION

*B*efore launching into your own planning process, it is important to have read and discussed definitions and examples of learning expeditions with colleagues. Explore your own definitions of the components of a learning expedition. Read and discuss narratives by teachers collected in *Journeys Through Our Classrooms* (eds. Mednick and Udall), comparing them with your own teaching situation. Critique the sample learning expedition plans contained in this booklet.

Ideally, you have also had a chance to observe and experience what a learning expedition will be like for your students. Visits to other Expeditionary Learning schools, participation in community explorations, interactive workshops, site seminars, and week-long summits (learning expeditions for educators) provide much more tangible illustrations of learning expeditions in action.

Key Elements of a Learning Expedition Plan:
Topic
What is the area of study around which the expedition can be built?

Guiding questions
What large question(s) will spark students' interests and inquiry and guide them on a journey into important content, concepts, and skills?

Learning goals

What will students understand and be able to do after they have completed the expedition? How will standards shape the development of goals and the plan as a whole?

Projects

What activities will help students develop the understanding and abilities reflected in the learning goals, and demonstrate what they have learned and are able to do? What practices should the teacher use to guide students through the expedition so that each and every student accomplishes the learning goals? What anticipated sequence of projects and activities will enable students to meet the learning goals (their own as well as the teacher's)?

Ongoing assessment

How will students know and demonstrate what they understand and can do? How will teachers and students reflect on the ways in which they have accomplished the learning goals? Ongoing assessment enables students to improve the quality of their work through reflection and revision.

Final assessment

How will teachers and students know whether they have met the goals of the expedition? By what standards will teachers and students assess learning and define quality work and achievement?

In planning a learning expedition, people often look at and think about each of these interconnected parts one at a time. But an expedition is far more than the sum of its parts, and in planning an expedition it is important to focus on how the parts relate to each other and fit together to create a powerful learning experience.

Perhaps the most important question to ask is "Why teach this?" What is so compelling about the topic that it will motivate teachers and students to work as hard as they will need to in order to be successful?

In the following pages, each component of the learning expedition is outlined and described. As you develop a plan, draw on these descriptions for ideas and direction, but do not feel limited by them. Although the components are presented in a sequence (Topics, Guiding Questions, Learning Goals, Projects, Assessment), planning almost never happens in a straight line. An idea for an expedition may come from a provocative question, an idea for a project, or a clear set of learning goals.

The most effective professional development in planning and teaching learning expeditions will balance individual learning with collaboration. If possible, it is best not to venture into this process completely on your own. The work is complex and challenging. A team of supportive colleagues, with whom you can share ideas, problem-solve, and divide tasks, is invaluable. Also, allow room for students to collaborate in the planning process by bringing their own goals, questions, and ideas to the table.

The suggested sequence for planning, outlined here and detailed in the pages that follow, assumes such a collaborative process.

OUTLINE OF A SEQUENCE
FOR PLANNING

Selecting a Topic

Keeping a Running List of Resources

Creating an Idea Map or Web

Creating an Outline or Sequence of Ideas

Proceeding from Four Different Points:
   1. Guiding Questions
   2. Learning Goals and Standards
   3. Projects
   4. Final Assessment

*Planning a Project in Detail, Including
Ongoing Assessment*

Creating a Calendar/Timeline for the Expedition

Completing the Written Planning Outline

*Planning, Revision, and Follow-up Throughout
the Expedition*

Final Reflection, Revision, and Documentation

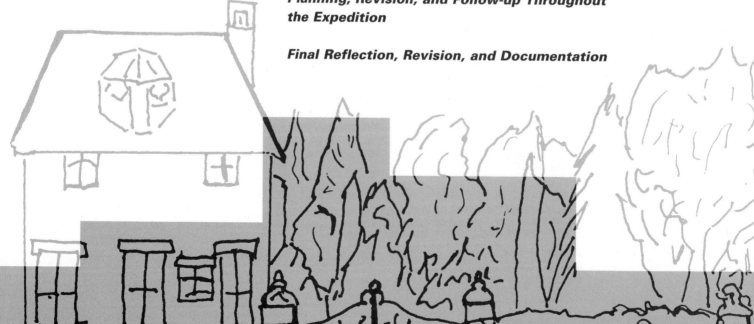

A SEQUENCE FOR PLANNING

Selecting a Topic

Brainstorm a list of possible topics. To do this effectively, consider all or some of the following:

~ Consider the definition, qualities, and criteria for good topics (p. 19)

~ Review your standards and curriculum frameworks

~ Look at examples of learning expedition plans and other curricula from your grade level

~ Reflect on your passions, areas of expertise, and experiences

After brainstorming a list of five to ten possibilities, discuss the pros and cons. As part of the discussion, consider the curriculum standards for your discipline or grade level. Which topics will allow you the greatest opportunity to teach to the standards?

Before making a tentative decision, revisit the qualities and examples of good topics. Which topic on your list comes closest to these criteria?

Keeping a Running List of Resources

Keep an ongoing list of books and other resources during your planning. Post it on a wall and record ideas as they come up. Invite colleagues and others to give their suggestions for the following:

~ Reading material: fiction and nonfiction books, short stories, articles, poems, etc.

~ Fieldwork and service sites or resources

~ "Experts" and other people who might be speakers, presenters, collaborators, etc.

~ Project materials you will need: art supplies, technology, science equipment, etc.

Creating an Idea Map or Web

Select the most promising topic and, as a team, create an idea web. Use a large sheet of newsprint and create a "messy" web of ideas, questions, activities, projects, learning goals, resources, and so on that might grow from the topic. At this brainstorming stage, it is important not to limit the flow of ideas.

After completing the web, decide as a team whether to move ahead with planning a learning expedition on this topic, or to create another web for a different topic.

Sample Web

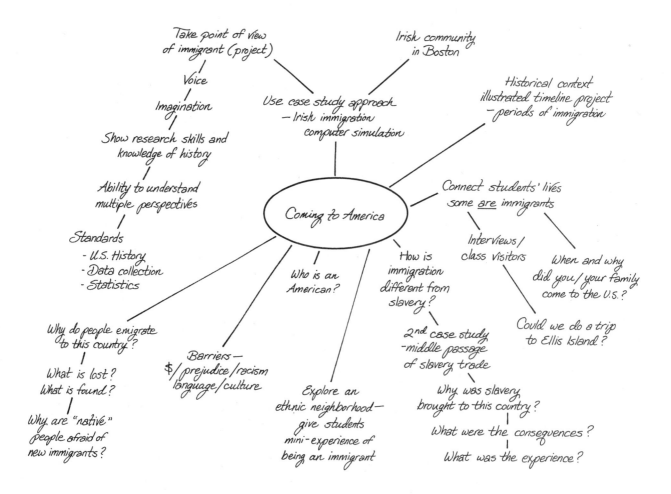

Creating an Outline or Sequence of Ideas

Next, once you are satisfied with your topic and brainstorming map or web, organize the main ideas and concepts into a rough sequence. Do not be concerned about whether they are learning goals, project ideas, or guiding questions. Just think about an order that makes sense.

In the following example drawn from the sample web, there is still a lot of detail to be worked out, but the expedition begins to take shape with a beginning, middle, and end.

Example of an idea sequence: Coming to America

1. Introduction: Why do people come to the United States? What are their struggles and what do they gain? (Read short stories such as "The All-American Slurp," by Lensey Namioka, and "Alien Turf," from *Down These Mean Streets,* by Piri Thomas.)

2. The immigrant experience in our own school community: panel discussion with Haitians in the school

3. Community exploration of Chinatown: What is a culture? What is a community? How did this community form?

4. Who is an American? Again, why and how did people come here?

5. What were their experiences, losses, and gains?

6. How did their communities form? What forces affected them?

7. What effect did these communities have on U.S. culture and community?

8. Create a large timeline of historical waves of immigration.

9. Irish immigration case study: "Immigrant 1850" computer simulation; diary project

10. African American experience case study: Read *To Be a Slave*; African American diary project (contrast between slavery and immigration).

11. How do we build a multicultural society? Present-day issues

12. Assimilation versus separatism

13. Immigration laws

14. Affirmative action

15. Fair housing writing contest

16. Final project: To be determined (Possibility: a handbook for local immigrants?)

Proceeding from Four Different Points: Guiding Questions, Learning Goals and Standards, Projects, Final Assessment

Determine whether to work next on Guiding Questions, Learning Goals and Standards, a Major Project, or a Final Assessment: Performance or Presentation of Learning. These four elements are the backbone of the learning expedition, and need to be closely aligned. It does not matter in what order they are developed, as long as they reinforce each other. (Note: each of the four elements is defined and illustrated in pp. 21–32.)

Go through a brainstorming process for each element—Guiding Questions, Learning Goals, Projects, and Final Assessment—in whatever order you choose.

After brainstorming, discuss the lists, drawing on the questions for each element (pp. 19–30). Choose priorities (your top ten goals, top two or three guiding questions, and so on), and be sure the four elements are aligned. In reality, planning is a messy, individual process. Some people proceed in an orderly, linear fashion through the components of the expedition, while others jump from one component to the next and back again.

Planning a Project in Detail, Including Ongoing Assessment

Once you have decided on the major projects for the expedition, choose the most important, or the first, and begin to plan it in more detail. What are the steps and activities that will lead to its completion? Start thinking about ongoing assessment in more detail.

Working on some of the specific ongoing assessment tools can help to flesh out your project plans and ensure their academic rigor, as the examples here illustrate.

Examples of assessment tools

- Criteria lists and/or rubrics, or a plan to involve students in their creation

- Journal prompts

- Self-assessment sheets

- Portfolio requirements

- Checklists and/or teacher observation log

Creating a Calendar/Timeline for the Expedition

Create a rough calendar/timeline for the expedition, including tentative dates for fieldwork, deadlines for projects, and a date for the final assessment—performance, publication, or demonstration.

Completing the Written Planning Outline

As the last step, complete the written planning outline, copying the form that begins on page 33, or creating your own format on the computer.

Consider that this document will be most useful if it is understandable to parents and other members of the community. A brief synopsis of your plan can be helpful. Also, you may find it useful to summarize your expedition using the Learning Expedition Plan Overview on page 44.

Considerations:

∼ Does your calendar reflect a *sequence* of activities and projects that will lead students to gain a deep understanding of the topic and guiding questions? Does the sequence reflect the beginning, middle, and final stages of an expedition? (For example, beginning with brainstorming and small experiments, progressing to guided drafting and revision in a longer project, and culminating with a more independent challenge.)

∼ Reflect on the plan as a whole. Will the learning expedition guide and help students attain the standards? Are the assessment activities planned sufficient to tell you and the students whether they have attained the standards? Make any necessary revisions to the plan.

∼ Remember that the outline is only one step in the ongoing planning process. Determine what remains to be done before beginning the expedition and assign tasks.

Planning, Revision, and Follow-up Throughout the Expedition

As the expedition unfolds during the school year, teams need regular meeting time to review progress, continue to develop, and adjust plans. In addition to the necessary nuts and bolts of planning—scheduling fieldwork, making sure there are enough copies of things, and so forth—several kinds of team meeting agendas are very helpful:

∼ Reflecting on what is working and not working as you teach the expedition.

∼ Sharing examples of student work produced during the expedition and reflecting on what it reveals about students' learning. Are we meeting the standards?

∼ Discussing new information to assist your work with expeditions—visits to other classrooms within and outside your school, curriculum narratives from other teachers, articles from professional journals, and so on.

Build in time during classes for conversations with students about how the expedition is going. Their questions and ideas may push the expedition in new directions.

Communicate with parents and community members as often as you can, seeking their ideas and input as well as thanking them for support. Be sure to have students write thank-you notes to visitors and fieldwork sites for the help provided during the expedition.

At one school, teachers take the time to reflect on past, present, and future strategies and activities. This weekly plan motivates the teachers to think about their instructional practice.

Reflective lesson plan

1. How did it go? Were my goals reached? (Reflect on the previous week.)

2. What I plan to do this week. (Includes specific or general strategies.)

3. Metacognition on my planning. (Reflect on your planning.)

4. Reflections on the Design Principles.

Final Reflection, Revision, and Documentation

After the expedition has been completed, teams need time to reflect on the quality of the expedition as a whole, and to make revisions in their plans. This is an often overlooked but critical part of the process. It requires a structure for providing teachers with time and/or compensation for the additional work involved, and most schools do not have this structure in place. However, without it, a dangerous pattern of reinventing the wheel develops, and schools have little opportunity to build on and learn from their experience as they teach expeditions again or plan new ones.

The process for teachers to engage in reflection, revision, and documentation is similar to the process of building a portfolio: Collect, Select, and Reflect. Depending on the time allotted and the goals, the following steps can be shortened and kept very simple, or extended into a more ambitious project:

Collect

Throughout the expedition collect student work and teacher materials (including daily or weekly plans) to help you document the expedition for your own and others' future use. Some people keep an accordion file, others a large binder. Include everything you believe might be useful later: copies of readings and assignment sheets, criteria, names and numbers of experts or fieldwork sites, photographs of a project exhibition, etc. Keeping a journal of your reflections on the progress of the expedition is very helpful. Even writing for as little as twenty to thirty minutes once a week will provide you with a valuable record of your thinking throughout the expedition. If all team members keep journals, the possibilities for learning are even greater.

Select

After the expedition is complete, review the collection of materials and create a "teaching portfolio" of the learning expedition. Pull out the items you think best illustrate the strengths and areas for improvement of the expedition. Organize the contents of the portfolio to tell the story of the expedition in a way that will be understandable to another teacher.

Reflect

Drawing on the definitions and examples provided in this guide, as well as Expeditionary Learning's *Core Practice Benchmarks,* reflect on the expedition's overall strengths and weaknesses. Decide whether you would choose to teach this particular expedition again. Revise your planning outline to reflect your experience and your analysis of what you would change next time. Write a brief narrative that incorporates reflections from your journal and assesses the strengths and weaknesses of the expedition. The goals for this reflective writing are both to clarify your own thinking about your practice and to help someone else who might want to teach a similar expedition.

ELEMENTS OF A LEARNING EXPEDITION:
DEFINITIONS AND EXAMPLES

TOPICS

The focus and content of the learning expedition should include the most important ideas and concepts from a discipline (or disciplines) that teachers believe all students must understand deeply. The topic defines an area rich enough to support prolonged study, but small enough to be explored in depth. Topics such as "Change and Progress" are broader, unifying themes, while ones like "Frogs" are more concrete. Powerful learning expeditions can be organized around either type. In selecting a good topic, there is sometimes an initial tension between what is most compelling to teachers and students, and what will explicitly meet local or state standards. Probe, examine, and question the topic until you are satisfied that it will allow the expedition to be both academically rigorous and engaging to students and teachers, while meeting state and local standards.

When selecting a topic, consider the following questions:

~ What background knowledge and skills will students need to develop and use in order to produce strong work in the expedition?

~ What big ideas will students grapple with? Are those ideas important to know?

~ Will students have the opportunity to use different modes of inquiry?

~ How will the topic lead to, or be strongly linked with, the questions that drive the expedition and push students' thinking?

~ How does the topic reflect central ideas and concepts from a discipline or disciplines?

~ How will it connect to students' and teachers' experiences and interests?

~ How will the topic allow the expedition to meet the standards and expectations of the school, district, or state?

~ How will it allow the learning expedition to encompass more than one discipline and make connections across fields of knowledge or experience?

~ How will it encourage perspective-taking, and the exploration of different cultures?

Examples of topics

Frogs	The American Revolution
Bicycles	Life on the Mississippi
Architecture	Activism and Community
Movement	Involvement
Galileo	Change and Progress
Transportation	Amazon Rain Forest
Pond Life	Puerto Rican History and Culture
	Urban Design and Infrastructure

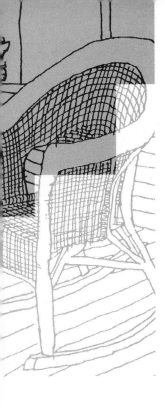

GUIDING QUESTIONS

Guiding questions engage students' interests and curiosity. Closely linked to learning goals, they also organize an expedition by providing students a way of approaching challenging subject matter.

As teachers plan learning expeditions, they create several guiding questions to shape the expedition and sharpen the focus of the topic. As an expedition begins, students are invited into the process, reshaping the original questions. Together, they discover new ideas while brainstorming a range of questions that interest or puzzle them, from the very concrete (Why do teeth fall out?) to complex and layered (Why did people let the Holocaust happen?). Throughout the expedition, teachers help the students think about which questions to explore and which to drop or postpone, balancing students' interests with the learning goals of the expedition. Involving students in developing questions not only builds their engagement in the expedition, it also teaches them the skills and habits of inquiry.

Although guiding questions will differ across developmental levels, many good questions are universal and can be explored at different grade levels. For example, the question "When is change progress?" is used to shape a series of middle school expeditions focused on American history. It might also be a powerful question for a fourth- or fifth-grade expedition with a science focus.

When developing guiding questions, consider the following questions:

∼ How will the guiding questions engage students' curiosity and wonder?

∼ What other questions will they lead to?

∼ How will the guiding questions ask students to investigate an interesting problem or dilemma, or make a decision about an important issue or problem?

∼ How will they challenge students to think critically and probe ideas deeply?

∼ What are the important ideas, problems, and methods of inquiry at the heart of a discipline, or a domain of knowledge, that the guiding questions will lead students to explore?

∼ How are the guiding questions connected to the learning goals?

∼ Are the guiding questions open-ended and provocative?

- What do you need to know to be a cat? ("Cats," second grade)

- What are the strategies people use in the face of hardship? ("1934/The Great Depression," ninth grade)

- When is change progress? (A yearlong guiding question for expeditions focused on wars and social movements in U.S. history, seventh and eighth grade)

- How do birds fly? ("Investigations," fifth grade)

LEARNING GOALS

Learning expeditions are designed and planned with clear learning goals. These goals are developed with district and state standards in mind—what students should understand and be able to do when they have completed the expedition. Some learning goals come from the students themselves, reflecting their interests, goals, and questions. The topic, guiding questions, projects, and culminating products and performances are designed to enable students to achieve these explicit learning goals.

Learning goals are divided into three basic categories:

Content
What knowledge, content, and concepts will students understand and be able to apply in new situations?

Skills and Habits
What skills and habits will they practice and be able to do?

Qualities of Character and Community
What qualities of character and service to others will students have practiced and demonstrated as individuals and groups?

When developing learning goals, consider the following questions:

~ How are the learning goals linked to district and state standards, and built around the core concepts, key ideas, tools, and thinking approaches of major disciplines?

~ Which goals will foster deep understanding (using and applying knowledge and skills in new situations) and ask students to be scientists or historians (not just to learn about science or history)?

~ Which goals incorporate essential skills, including critical thinking and problem solving?

~ Are the goals reachable but challenging, asking students to go beyond their perceived limits?

~ In what ways are the goals developmental, age-appropriate, and built on what students already know?

~ How will students be encouraged and helped in creating their own learning goals?

~ Are the goals explicit? Do they give students a clear understanding of what they are supposed to accomplish?

Content Goals

These are concepts, ideas, and facts students will know and understand.

**Examples of content goals
(illustrating both content and its application)**

- Seventh-grade students learn the concepts of survey research, mean and median, perimeter and area, design, and the political process. Students apply what they have learned to determine community priorities for the reuse of three vacant lots, and create a drawn-to-scale design and model for the reuse of one lot. They use the political process to get a vacant lot redeveloped using their design. ("Urban Structures," seventh and eighth grade)

- Tenth-grade students learn the principles of quadratic equations and factoring as they design and sketch a fountain, and collaboratively design and build a fountain for the school. Students apply the math they learn to calculate the height and width of the water arc, angles, and water speed, and to create equations and graphs of the arc. ("Quadratic Equations," tenth grade)

- First-grade students learn the different forms and modes of transportation, and how they work together in a city. They also learn the fundamentals of mapping. They apply what they have learned in planning and building a model city. ("Transportation," first grade)

Skills and Habits Goals

Students will practice and be able to:

~ view issues, problems, and questions from a variety of perspectives

---

Example of viewing from another perspective

In their investigation of the experience of the Cherokee, students take on the character of a key historical figure. Regardless of their own feelings about their figure's views and actions, the students stay in character as they write and perform a role-play negotiation of the Treaty of New Echota. ("The Cherokee Experience," fifth and sixth grade)

~ distinguish between fact and inference, and use facts to test theories

~ justify and defend ideas, answers, and solutions

~ draw upon prior knowledge and creatively use what they know in new situations

~ examine relationships between different ideas, people, concepts, and phenomena, make connections, and understand cause and effect

~ ask probing questions and follow the trail of inquiry as each question leads to others

~ conduct research using multiple kinds of sources to create strong written and oral work

Character and Community Goals

Students will practice and develop qualities of character and service to community.

They will:

~ seek to understand other people's ideas, and look at their own ideas from other perspectives

~ demonstrate compassion, caring, and service to others

Example of demonstrating compassion, caring and service

Sixth-grade students spend time getting to know and interviewing a resident of a nursing home. They write biographies of the residents and present them as gifts. ("Life Stories," sixth grade)

~ collaborate well with others and give and receive effective and constructive feedback

~ take risks, pursue high standards of craftsmanship and academic excellence, and learn from mistakes

~ resolve conflict constructively

Example of conflict resolution

Middle school students engaged in designing architectural models in a collaborative team get into a vigorous dispute over which student's idea to use. After much debate they modify an idea and move ahead. ("Urban Structures," seventh and eighth grade)

PROJECTS

Learning expeditions are built around projects. Good projects give students a compelling reason to learn and foster in-depth understanding by asking students to do real work that is meaningful and important. Great projects require a stretch of imagination and effort on the part of everyone. They are the major vehicle for learning important content, skills, and habits, as well as for developing qualities of character. Projects confront students with real-world problems and dilemmas that require them to use the approaches, tools, language, and standards used by professionals in the world outside of school. They motivate students to do their best work, providing opportunities for them to present their work before audiences.

Learning expeditions may include a series of smaller projects, sometimes culminating in an "expedition portfolio," or in a single, complex project. Most complex projects are made up of a series of different activities and tasks that lead to a final product or performance that has value beyond the school. To reach opening night of a play, for example, a class must research the topic; debate; study a variety of plays and think about the qualities of a good play; think about the issues, characters, and content of the play; develop a script, revising it many times; rehearse until the play is good enough to perform; and put on the final performance for family and other community members.

When planning projects, consider the following questions:

~ How will the project provide a compelling answer to the question "Why do we need to learn this anyway?" Is it challenging yet doable?

~ How is it aligned with the expedition's learning goals, and will it allow students to demonstrate the most significant things they have learned?

~ What are the real-world problems, issues, or questions that the students will face during a project? How will it require them to understand and use the approaches, concepts, thinking strategies, and tools of different disciplines that professionals outside of school would use to solve those problems?

~ How will the project require students to use tools of inquiry, research, experimentation, interpreting original documents, collecting and analyzing data, distinguishing between fact and inference, and looking at things from different perspectives? How will it include a variety of means of expression—written, oral, artistic, physical, and mathematical?

～ How will the expedition balance group and individual tasks, allowing individual students to stretch beyond their limits while developing teamwork skills?

～ Are the tasks within the project explicit and clearly defined so that students know exactly what they are supposed to do and understand the standards for good work?

～ How will the project be structured so that it fosters strong work habits such as perseverance, organization, planning and follow-through, craftsmanship, imagination, and self-discipline?

～ As they work on the project, how will students engage by using a rich variety of sources: books, models, experiments, expert speakers, poetry, hands-on math applications, primary documents and sources, paintings, music, and computer software?

～ What purposeful fieldwork will support the students' research and work on the project?

Examples of projects

- To learn and practice skills of literacy and revision, as well as acquire knowledge of health and nutrition, first graders write a manual that other kindergarten and first-grade students can use to plan and participate in a camping trip. The manual discusses what food to bring and how to cook it, weather conditions and what clothing to bring, and how to set up a tent. Students field-test the manual on a camping trip to see whether another student can do the task using their directions, and then make revisions. ("The Natural World," first grade)

- In a project focused on social studies and math content, seventh graders survey the community around their school to find out how community members would like to see vacant lots used. They use the data to formulate proposals and write letters to public officials. Using actual measurements, students design plans to redevelop a lot and build a scale model of their design. Students present their designs before a community audience and city agencies, explaining the reasons why

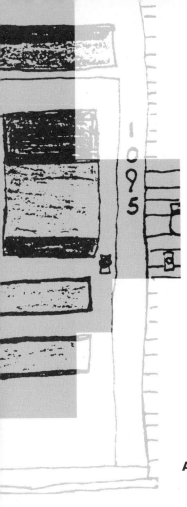

their design should be used to redevelop one of the vacant lots in the community. ("Urban Structures," seventh and eighth grade)

- As part of an astronomy expedition, high school students conduct observations and research within the scientific and technological constraints of Galileo's time. They build a telescope like Galileo's and use it to observe Jupiter and its moons. They also read about Galileo's life and his observations, the lives of other important astronomers, and the art and literature of the time. Students use these sources to put themselves in Galileo's place and to discover the consequences and implications of seeing Jupiter's moons. To synthesize and present what they have learned, students write an essay about what Galileo saw when he looked at Jupiter, and explain what that observation shows about how the solar system may work. ("Galileo," tenth grade)

ASSESSMENT

Assessment is ongoing and embedded in the process of the learning expedition. The primary purpose of assessment is to give feedback on student learning to the teacher and student. Assessment also provides feedback to the teacher on the effectiveness of instruction and curriculum design. As teachers and students reflect on student work and assess it, they should refer to learning goals and standards and ask themselves, "Are we there yet?"

In this vision of assessment, there are not many secrets or surprises for the student. Students know the standards and criteria for important projects and tasks before they begin an expedition. Often teachers and students create and revise criteria together. Assessment activities that make use of standards and criteria take many forms, from guided self-assessment, to group critique, to the creation of portfolios. A portfolio is often the anchor of ongoing assessment within a learning expedition. Students collect all drafts of their work, reflect on the work's strengths and weaknesses, and select what belongs in the portfolio. In this process, opportunities for

assessment are opportunities for reflection and learning. Along the way, and at the end of the expedition, students share their work and demonstrate their understanding for outside audiences.

When planning ongoing assessment activities that take place throughout an expedition, consider the following questions:

~ How will assessment provide opportunities for students to assess and evaluate their work against clear standards that they understand?

~ What are the models, and what is the process for examining them, and developing criteria that will help students understand the qualities of good work?

~ How will the expedition promote a culture of revision, asking students to create multiple drafts of important products?

~ How will critique sessions, peer review, and conferences be organized to give students feedback to improve their work?

~ What strategies will be used to have students collect their work throughout the expedition, and spend time on individual reflection and self-assessment using the criteria developed in the class?

~ At what points in the expedition will teachers have opportunities to reflect on students' understanding and make adjustments to their practice?

~ How will students share their work with each other and many different kinds of audiences?

When planning final assessment activities that take place at the close of an expedition, consider the following questions:

~ How will students be asked to select work from the expedition for their portfolios?

~ What final reflection format will allow the student and teacher to assess the learning that took place over the course of the whole expedition? How will standards be addressed in this final assessment?

~ What exhibition, demonstration, performance, or portfolio review will give students a chance to knit together what they have learned throughout the expedition and demonstrate their understanding to an outside audience? How will standards be addressed during this culminating performance or review?

Examples of assessment activities embedded in learning expeditions

- During a learning expedition on South America, a seventh-grade class examined models of children's books from last year's class to develop criteria lists and rubrics for their own children's books. Their books would teach second-grade students about South American history and culture. A visiting illustrator helped the class to create criteria for illustrations. After they completed the first drafts of their books, students participated in a structured critique session in which they followed a protocol to comment on each other's work. Subsequent drafts were similarly critiqued by teacher and peers. When the books were ready, the older students read their books to the younger children and assessed the books' interest and readability. They wrote a final self-assessment of their work on the project, and decided whether to include the book in their language arts portfolio.

- In a first-grade classroom, working folders for learning expeditions were kept nearby, so that students may collect all drafts of work and have access to them. During their expedition on "The Natural World," the students wrote drafts of camping manuals and then tested them during an actual camping trip. Back in the classroom they discussed what had worked and not worked when they tried to use the manuals. They made revisions to the content and organization of the books and published final versions for use in future classes. Throughout the expedition, the teacher focused on the literacy development of her students, and observed and recorded their progress in important skill areas.

- A twelfth-grade class conducted independent research projects investigating a question that each individual had about New York City. The questions emerged from the students' experience at a city internship, and from an

exploration of the design principles, which students adapted to apply to a civic community. After completing the final draft, each student gave a half-hour presentation to an audience of friends of the school, internship supervisors, and other community people in a college conference room and at the conference of the Credit Suisse institution. The audience responded with questions and feedback.

Learning Expedition
Planning Outline

TOPIC

GUIDING QUESTIONS

LEARNING GOALS
Refer to state and district standards when creating Learning Goals.

Students will understand...
(knowledge of content)

Students will practice and be able to do...
(skills and habits)

Students will practice and develop qualities of character and community, including...

PROJECTS
A learning expedition may include one major, or a few smaller, projects

PROJECT DESCRIPTION

_____
_____
_____
_____
_____
_____
_____
_____
_____
_____

LEARNING GOALS ADDRESSED BY PROJECT
(Refer to relevant goals from preceding page)

_____
_____
_____
_____
_____
_____
_____
_____
_____

MAJOR ACTIVITIES/STEPS (Steps leading to the completion of the project)	SPECIFIC GOALS FOR ACTIVITIES/STEPS (Refer to state and district standards. These may be more specific goals than overall learning goals.)

MAJOR ACTIVITIES/
STEPS (cont.)
(Steps leading to the completion of the project)

SPECIFIC GOALS FOR
ACTIVITIES/STEPS (cont.)
(Refer to state and district standards. These may be more specific goals than overall learning goals.)

ONGOING ASSESSMENT
(Specific strategies you intend to use within this project)

ASSESSMENT

FINAL ASSESSMENT: PERFORMANCE
OR PRESENTATION OF LEARNING
(Describe assessment of group or individual projects such as debates, galleries, exhibits of work, oral presentations of portfolios of project work, play performances, or final essays and research papers)

ASSESSING STUDENTS' OVERALL ACHIEVEMENT
(By what standards will you and the students assess learning and define quality work and achievement on the learning expedition as a whole?)

RESOURCES
Develop a list of resources that will anchor the content of the expedition, including books, speakers, "experts," fieldwork sites, project materials, and so on

BOOKS, ARTICLES, LITERATURE
(Select titles for required and optional reading)

EXPERTS
(Who are the experts who could help plan, visit the classroom, or be contacted by individual students?)

FIELDWORK SITES

(What sites can be visited by the whole class and/or small groups of students?)

PROJECT MATERIALS AND EQUIPMENT

LEARNING EXPEDITION
PLAN OVERVIEW

TOPIC	PROJECTED TIMELINE

TEAM MEMBERS	BOOKS

GUIDING QUESTIONS

LEARNING GOALS
(Refer to standards)

_____

_____

_____

_____

_____

PROJECTS	FIELDWORK, RESOURCES, SERVICES

DISCIPLINES INVOLVED	ONGOING AND FINAL ASSESSMENT

NEXT STEPS

Narrative

Write a brief narrative overview of your learning expedition plan (two to three paragraphs). Attach it at the beginning of the completed planning guide.

Timeline

Determine a timeline or calendar for the learning expedition, with projected deadlines for projects. This should reflect a sequence of activities and projects that will lead students to gain a deep understanding of the topic and guiding questions.

Immersion

Create an opening or immersion activity to spark students' interest. (For example, a learning expedition on the Great Depression began with an immersion day into the popular culture of the 1930s.)

Service

If one of your projects is not explicitly a "service project," consider other ways of incorporating the ethic and practice of service into the learning expedition.

Parents

Plan for informing and including parents. Some teachers choose to write a letter to parents describing the learning expedition and asking for ideas or assistance.

Design Principles

Re-read the ten design principles in light of your outline. How will these principles be incorporated into the learning expedition? Do any need concrete attention or planning?

Reflections

Review your plan: Will the learning expedition guide and help students to attain high standards for character and intellectual development? Are the assessment activities planned sufficient to tell you and the students whether they have attained these standards and expectations? Make any necessary revisions to the plan.

Continuous Improvement

Build in time weekly for ongoing planning, making midcourse corrections, or refining.

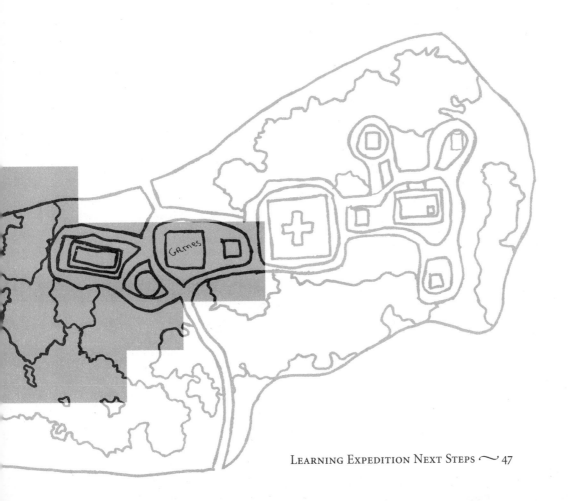

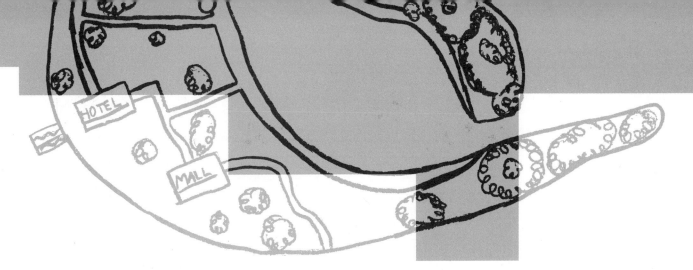

LEARNING EXPEDITION NARRATIVES AND PLAN OUTLINES

INTRODUCTION

*I*n this section, we have collected six narratives of learning expeditions with their accompanying plan outlines, written by experienced Expeditionary Learning teachers. In microcosm, these expeditions represent the diversity within the Expeditionary Learning network. They range from first grade through high school and address a variety of topics and subject area focuses. All of the teachers have been teaching in an Expeditionary Learning school for at least three years, and several for five. Some came to Expeditionary Learning as relatively new teachers, while others were already veterans when their schools took on the design. Geographically the expeditions cover the map: Dubuque, Iowa; Decatur, Georgia; Portland, Maine; New York City; and Denver, Colorado.

At first we thought that the teacher-writers would follow the plan outline format very strictly. As the process evolved, however, we saw the strength in the individual ways people captured their planning and teaching. Together, the collection illustrates the common core of all of the elements of a learning expedition and the freedom with which individual teachers and their students adapt and use them.

Each of the narratives reflects on the teacher's or teaching team's experience with the learning expedition. The planning outlines are not the original plans, but were created retrospectively to reflect what the teachers learned from what actually occurred. We hope they will be useful not only as a rich source of ideas for future learning expeditions, but also as a model for documenting and reflecting on curriculum and teaching.

We strongly encourage all Expeditionary Learning teachers to write about their learning expeditions, and to share those reflections across their schools and across our network. We look forward to refining the process and continuing to publish collections of these narrative reflections. Please send us your suggestions and your works-in-progress so we may learn together.

Scientific Revolution:
Galileo's New View

JONATHAN MANN
Rocky Mountain School of Expeditionary Learning
Denver, Colorado

O ye men of Galilee, why stand ye gazing up into heaven?

*I*magine offering a picture of our universe that you are convinced, by observation, is accurate while those around you stand in disbelief. Imagine arousing the anger of the powers that be as you try to convince them of the true structure of their world. Imagine being imprisoned for your ideas. This was the fate of Galileo Galilei (1564–1642) during the bright rise of the Italian Renaissance and dark cloud of the Inquisition.

During this tenth-grade physics and astronomy expedition students explored the events that motivated Galileo to offer his radical new picture of the universe. They read and relived Galileo's original observations of Jupiter and the moon by reproducing and using Galileo's original telescope to investigate light and the mechanics of the telescope and lenses. They used the models of Aristotle, Ptolemy, and Copernicus to compare with Galileo's model of the solar system. And, finally, they investigated the nature of revolution and the use of technology as an agent for change. The depth of content in art, science, literature, math, and the culture of the time also allowed for valuable "side trips." Our school director, Rob Stein, graced us with an amazing Renaissance art show that required all of us to grapple with the impact of science on painting. Unintentionally, algebra became the method to solve problems of magnification, focal point, and object distances of our telescopes. We stuck to a strict constructivist method, however, to build our understanding of the moon's phases.

For me, creating and implementing expeditions has been a process of trial and error—revise, and go at it again. It is this expedition, surprisingly on the first try, that gave me a working format for other expeditions that followed. The simple focus of the telescope, the richness of Renaissance art and ideas, and the impact of the discovery of objects in motion around Jupiter made this a success. Students were engaged because they built their understanding of the concepts from experience. They understood Galileo's radical observations and interpretations because they read and argued about what he wrote. They saw how lenses work because they built a working telescope, and they were able to visualize the phases of the moon because they constructed mental models over several weeks of observation and discussion.

I learned a great deal during this experience. The power of primary resources to bring the reader to an understanding of and feeling for the time and place was essential. I was a novice at telescope building and became a learner taught by the students who came across inventive ways to make it work. This project was the glue that held us together. I got a chance to really take a stab at a constructivist method in which students build their own understanding of a concept. And this expedition was built upon an exciting time period during which religion and science began to clash and advancement in our understanding of the universe took a leap forward. The questions about how the heavens and Earth moved relative to one another revolve around the telescope. It is this technology that made Galileo's story interesting, accessible, and relevant.

PLAN OUTLINE

TOPIC

Change/Scientific Revolutions

GUIDING QUESTIONS

~ Is technology responsible for revolutionary change?

~ Why were Galileo's observations so radical as to force the Church to imprison him?

~ How do lenses change the things we see?

~ How does the moon move about the Earth and what are lunar phases?

LEARNING GOALS

Knowledge and Content
Students will understand:

~ the use of the observations of the moons of Jupiter as the evidence of a new model of our solar system

~ Galileo's model in comparison with the models of Aristotle, Ptolemy, and Copernicus

~ Galileo's observations, changes, and conclusions

~ how a telescope enhances and focuses an upright image

~ how to draw lens diagrams that clearly show the image, object, lenses, focal points, and light lines to scale

~ lens calculations of focal lengths and magnification of the telescope

~ how to explain and define the movement and phases of Earth's moon

~ the scientific changes reflected in Renaissance art

Skills and Habits

Students will practice and be able to:

~ reflect about the ideas, techniques, and process used to create the telescope

~ write daily journal entries to support explanations

~ compare Galileo's discovery about Jupiter's moons to observations of earlier astronomers

Character and Community

Students will:

~ work closely with others as they build a telescope

~ use their own knowledge and that of their peers to create a model of the moon's phases

EXPEDITION SEQUENCE

1. Immersion

The immersion is the initial exposure, ideally intensive, that defines major questions and establishes the direction of the expedition. In order to demonstrate Galileo's level of inquiry, students will read the observations of Jupiter's moons in Galileo's *Starry Messenger,* excerpts from Shakespeare's writings, and biographies of Aristotle, Ptolemy, and Copernicus. The *Starry Messenger* text has been cut so that students will write the conclusion to his observations. The initial draft will be due on day one after reading only *Starry Messenger* and a brief biography of Galileo. Days two and three will involve small-group sessions that explore the work of Shakespeare, Aristotle, Ptolemy, and Copernicus, and include a visit to the Jeffco Planetarium for an overview of astronomy up to 1700. Revisions will begin after this gathering of additional information.

Task #1

You are Galileo. In your readings about Galileo's observations, his life, the lives of the earlier important astronomers, and the art and literature of the time, you should get a feel for the Italian Renaissance. Use these sources to think like Galileo and discover the consequences of seeing objects move

about Jupiter. Conclude, in writing, Galileo's chapter about what he saw when gazing at Jupiter. Explain what you (Galileo) saw and what it means about how the solar system may work.

Products

A revised written conclusion to the *Starry Messenger,* Galileo's translated observations, to reflect the consequence of these observations of the moons of Jupiter, connections to the development of his view of the solar system, and comparisons with earlier astronomers' solar system model.

Evidence of Understanding

~ The description of the moon's changes over time and the conclusion reached by Galileo

~ The use of the observations of the moons of Jupiter as the evidence of a new model of our solar system

~ A comparison of Galileo's model with those of Aristotle, Ptolemy, and Copernicus

Assessment

Teacher-developed rubric. See page 59.

2. Ground School/Main Stage

Ground school/main is the stage where more in-depth content work is done and the major project is completed. In this stage students will explore the technology of the time by recreating a Galilean telescope; analyze, by making lens diagrams and calculating magnification, how light behaves as it moves through lenses; and explain ways to make the telescope more powerful. In addition, students will create a written explanation and model of our moon's phases by nightly observations using their telescopes and naked eyes.

Task #2

You are Galileo. In groups of two, you will construct a Galilean telescope similar to the one that Galileo used in his observations. In addition, each student will need to create scale lens diagrams using the lenses available, and explain, in writing, the calculations for his or her telescope's magnification. The explanation should also include ways to make the telescope more powerful and useful for observing larger areas of the universe.

Products

A Galilean telescope, scale telescope lens diagrams with explanation, calculations for magnification, and a written reflection about the process and the final product.

Evidence of Understanding

∿ The telescope must enhance and focus an image upright

∿ The lens diagrams must clearly show the image, object, lenses, focal points, and light lines to scale

∿ Calculations must include focal lengths and magnification of the telescope

∿ Reflection must occur about the ideas, techniques, and process used to create the telescope

Assessment

Checklist using the above evidence for telescope and diagram, and a lens test. See page 61.

Task #3

Like Galileo, you will use your observations to explain the movement and appearance of the moon over a period of time. You should address these questions: Why does the moon's appearance change? What are the phases of the moon? What is periodic change?

Product

Written explanation and model about the movement of the moon around the Earth using evidence from observations of the moon in your Moon Journal.

Evidence of Understanding

∿ Daily journal entries are used to support explanations

∿ Movement and phases are explained and defined

∿ Comparison is made to Galileo's discovery about Jupiter's moons to observations of earlier astronomers

Assessment

Teacher-developed rubric. See page 62.

PERFORMANCE STANDARDS

Knowledge
Physical Science

~ Students will demonstrate knowledge, by creating lens diagrams of objects, images and magnification, and the properties of refraction

~ Students will demonstrate knowledge through calculating the magnification of a telescope using focal point and object size

Earth and Space Science

~ Students will demonstrate knowledge by describing evidence that supports past scientific theories about the model of our solar system

~ Students will demonstrate knowledge by explaining the movement and causes of the phases of the moon

Science, Technology, and Human Activity

~ Students will demonstrate their understanding of a major scientific event and the impact of the event on human society

Critical Thinking
Conducting Investigations

~ Students will draw conclusions and make predictions about the solar system using observations of the moons of Jupiter (Induction)

~ Students will investigate the consequences of what happened when Galileo used his telescope to observe the planets (Inquiry)

Recognizing Connections Between Science and the Real World

~ Students will demonstrate understanding by analyzing a major scientific event and its impact on human society

Communication
Explaining Theories, Ideas, and Procedures

∼ Students will demonstrate understanding by explaining the movement and causes of the phases of the moon

Interpreting and Challenging Information

∼ Students will demonstrate understanding by describing evidence that supports past scientific theories about the model of our solar system

Communicating with Purpose, Data, and Reasoning

∼ Students will demonstrate skills by describing evidence that supports past scientific theories about the model of our solar system

∼ Students will demonstrate understanding by analyzing a major scientific event and its impact on human society

Creativity
Invention of Tools and Techniques to Solve Problems

∼ Students will demonstrate understanding through reflection on the creation of techniques that helped create a working telescope

RESOURCES

The Discoveries and Opinions of Galileo, trans. by Stillman Drake (includes excerpt of *The Starry Messenger,* by Galileo Galilei). New York: Doubleday Anchor Books, 1957.

Hewitt, Paul. *Conceptual Physics.* New York: HarperCollins College Publishers, 1993.

Local planetarium. Ask the director if he or she will demonstrate the early views of the universe by Aristotle, Copernicus, Ptolemy, and Galileo.

Telescope-building guidelines and inquiry at http://www.galileo.rice.edu. This site will outline all the materials needed to create a telescope.

	Knowledge *Your work demonstrates*	Critical Thinking *Your work demonstrates*	Communication *Your work demonstrates*
Exemplary	• a thorough understanding of Galileo's observations, development of a new model of the solar system, and comparison with Aristotle, Ptolemy, and Copernicus that provides new insights into models of the solar system	• that you can conduct an investigation using important and unique information-gathering techniques • that you can interpret information accurately and in insightful ways	• that you can explain theories, ideas, and procedures clearly with sufficient support and rich, vivid, and powerful detail • that you can use effective techniques to communicate with purpose, data, and reasoning in a highly creative and insightful manner
Accomplished	• knowledge about Galileo's observations of Jupiter's moons that is accurate and complete • knowledge of Galileo's new model and its comparison with the thinking of Aristotle, Ptolemy, and Copernicus that is accurate and complete	• that you can conduct an investigation using information-gathering techniques • that you can interpret information accurately for this task	• that you can explain theories, ideas, and procedures clearly with sufficient support and detail • that you can use effective techniques to communicate with purpose, data, and reasoning

TASK #1 RUBRIC: SCIENTIFIC REVOLUTIONS (CONT.)

	Knowledge *Your work demonstrates*	Critical Thinking *Your work demonstrates*	Communication *Your work demonstrates*
Developing	• knowledge about Galileo's observations of Jupiter's moons that is incomplete and has some misconceptions • knowledge of Galileo's new model and its comparison with Aristotle, Ptolemy, and Copernicus that is incomplete and has some misconceptions	• that your investigation fails to use some significant information-gathering technique • that you make errors in interpreting information and synthesize it imprecisely	• that you can explain information but not with a clear theme or overall structure • that you attempt to communicate for a specific purpose but with errors in data and reasoning
Beginning	• knowledge about Galileo's observations of Jupiter's moons that has severe misconceptions • knowledge of Galileo's new model and its comparison with Aristotle, Ptolemy, and Copernicus that has severe misconceptions	• that your investigation fails to use an information-gathering technique • that you misinterpret the information gathered	• that you communicate information as isolated pieces in a random fashion • that you communicate without a central purpose or fail to articulate a purpose

1. Lens Practice Problems _____

2. Lens Activity

_____ Data table for various positions of image.

3. Telescope

_____ Enhances and focuses an image upright.

4. Lens Diagrams

_____ The original object, lenses, focal points, and light rays are present and labeled.

_____ The diagram is clear and concise, completed on graph paper.

_____ Calculations for image #1 and object #2 and magnification are accurate and clear.

5. Written Reflection

_____ Description of the process, difficulties, and learning that occurred are discussed.

Comments

_____

_____

TASK #3 RUBRIC: MOON JOURNAL (SEE PAGE 56.)

	Knowledge *Your work demonstrates*	Critical Thinking *Your work demonstrates*	Communication *Your work demonstrates*
Exemplary	• a thorough and accurate description of the moon's phases and its movement which includes details of your observations and explanations	• that you can conduct an investigation using important and unique information-gathering techniques • that you can interpret information accurately and in insightful ways	• that you can explain theories, ideas, and procedures clearly with sufficient support and rich, vivid, and powerful detail • that you can use effective techniques to communicate with purpose, data, and reasoning in a highly creative and insightful manner
Accomplished	• that phases of the moon and its movement are described accurately	• that you can conduct an investigation using information-gathering techniques • that you can interpret information accurately for this task	• that you can explain theories, ideas, and procedures clearly with sufficient support and detail • that you can use effective techniques to communicate with purpose, data, and reasoning

	Knowledge *Your work demonstrates*	Critical Thinking *Your work demonstrates*	Communication *Your work demonstrates*
Developing	• that your knowledge about the moon's phases and movement is incomplete and has some misconceptions	• that your investigation fails to use some significant information-gathering technique • that you make errors in interpreting information and synthesize it imprecisely	• that you can explain information but not with a clear theme or overall structure • that you attempt to communicate for a specific purpose but with errors in data and reasoning
Beginning	• that your knowledge about the moon's phases and movement has severe misconceptions	• that your investigation fails to use an information-gathering technique • that you misinterpret the information gathered	• that you communicate information as isolated pieces in a random fashion • that you communicate without a central purpose or fail to articulate a purpose

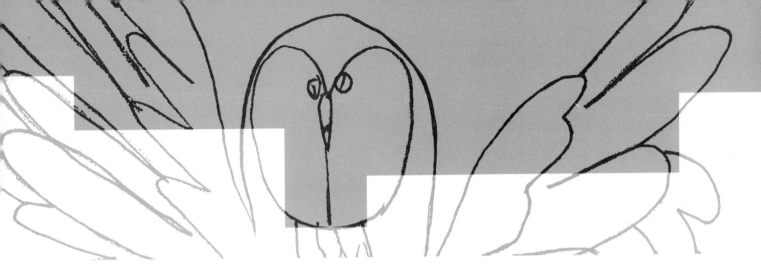

Immigration/Migration

VIVIAN STEPHENS
Clairemont School
Decatur, Georgia

*A*t the suggestion of a parent at my school, in the summer of 1996 I considered teaching an expedition on animal migration. But participating in the Civil Rights Summit taught me that people also migrate, and by fall it inspired me to broaden the learning expedition to include the immigration and migration of people, plants, and animals. I wanted to compare the migration patterns of plants and animals as well as help my fourth graders discover why migrants and immigrants came to the United States from other countries during the nineteenth century. The expedition also allowed us to learn about and discuss the impact of the differences among immigration, migration, and emigration. While expeditions usually lend themselves to either social studies or science, this expedition naturally integrated science, social studies, language arts, research, and art. It also covered state content standards for fourth grade, such as animal population, people and animals living in groups, parts of a plant, plant seed production, and classification of plants.

We discovered that people, plants, and animals migrate or immigrate as a matter of survival. Human beings travel from one place to another looking for a better way of life; some animals, such as the wildebeest, migrate and travel behind herds of other animals in search of food; and we learned that seeds dropped on a hard or sandy surface sit there, while a seed dropped on fertile ground will sprout if it has the resources it needs to germinate.

I concentrated more thoroughly on animals and people, sandwiching in a smaller—but rich in science—section on plants. I began with animal migration, showing the class the film *Serengeti* about animals migrating in Africa. They took notes on the animals, where they migrated to, and why they traveled. Each student selected an animal and began individual research for his or her main animal project, which the children decided would be publishing a written report in a professional and creative style, drawing the animal in its own habitat, and creating a model of each animal.

First, the children researched whether or not the animal they selected actually migrated, and as a result some children switched animals. In addition to the school library, where students learned to use the computer encyclopedia, we went to the public library as a class to gather additional resources. As they researched and found materials written for older children or adults, I would read sections of those books or articles aloud to the class, groups of students, or individuals, stopping often to ask questions or explain the text. While the children worked independently on this particular project, I gave them extra points for helping other students with their research. I encouraged the students to lend each other resources. For instance, one student might find at home or in the library a magazine article focusing on another child's animal. This way the students worked more collaboratively, and they became familiar with each animal under study.

After the children researched the animals' habitats, the art teacher taught the class a technique for drawing a silhouette of the animal with white chalk on black construction paper and then going over the lines with white glue to create a distinct outline. With pastels, they learned the technique of shading and blending to deepen the color and create a vibrant, accurate picture of the animal.

Meanwhile, I took the class to a folk art exhibit in Atlanta called "Souls Grown Deep," of the works of Southern artists of African American descent who had either migrated or immigrated. People had taken things such as discarded tin, tree roots, wood, or paper from their environment and turned it into art. A lawyer from Atlanta discovered a unique medium for sculpture as he remodeled his home. He took sawdust the carpenters generated each day and mixed it with wheat paste and glue to build very creative sculptures. We were so inspired that we decided to make our sculptures out of the same material. With the help of the art teacher, we created realistic

sculptures of the animals, painted them with poster paints, and covered them with a clear acrylic to produce a shine.

Throughout this time we worked on researching and writing the animal reports. The students had agreed during a class discussion to concentrate on the habitat of the animal, where it migrates, why it migrates, its gestation period, and the food it consumes. As part of the writing process, the media specialist taught them how to do research, paraphrase information, and take notes. They answered the specific questions generated as a class. I asked them to take notes on the collected materials, and make sure in the process to document their sources for their bibliographies. As the students completed their research, they began writing their reports: we wrote, we went through the critique process, and we revised. Inspired by student brochures from King Middle School in Portland, Maine, which I had seen presented at an Expeditionary Learning leadership retreat, I required that the students present the final, published report as a professional and unusual "brochure." For example, one child created a large elephant's head and fit the writing into the trunk in an accordion fold complete with an outline, bibliography, table of contents, and the body of the report. We laminated all the reports, which accompanied their sculptures and drawings.

PLANT MIGRATION

At the end of this intensive period of individual work, we gathered again as a class to talk about plants. I decided the children should work collaboratively as a group on a smaller, but rigorous project that immersed them in the science of plant migration. As I always do at the beginning of a large project, we generated a KWL chart, focusing on the questions what do you Know? what do you Want to know? and what have you Learned?

After I facilitated a brainstorming and discussion session, the students decided they wanted to learn how seeds get from one place to another. We decided to form four groups, each concentrating on three seeds that travel by animals, wind, water, and humans. In their groups, the students needed to answer the questions "Where do these plants travel?" "How do they travel?" and "What are the seeds that travel?" Three groups chose to portray this knowledge in a mural, and the group concentrating on seeds that travel by animals selected a board game as its project.

During this section of the expedition, I gave numerous "minilessons" (short teacher presentations): we learned about parts of a flower, seed development, and pollen grains that we looked at under a microscope. We ate seeds and learned the difference between monocots and dicots. I brought in peanuts, a clear example of dicots, and corn kernels, a good example of monocots. We also sprouted some seeds so that the children could see the difference in how monocots and dicots sprouted. We looked at plants the wind carries, such as dandelions, and walked on the trail in back of our school to collect examples.

The children did the research necessary to answer the questions and figured out among themselves who showed the greatest talent in sketching, painting, writing, organizing, or word processing. Three of the groups created ten-foot-long pastel murals that depicted the life of a seed. The group that did the board game asked questions illustrating what they had learned. For instance, they asked, "What kinds of seeds might specific animals move?" (Burrs that got stuck in the fur of an animal.)

IMMIGRATION AND MIGRATION OF PEOPLE

At the end of this varied but intensive science section, we were ready to begin relating this topic to people. As a kickoff activity I asked the children to draw their own shoes as a way to celebrate diversity and to point out a historical means of transportation and migration. We also constructed personal maps that showed how each student came to live in Decatur. Again, as a group, the students generated their questions in a KWL (what do you Know? what do you Want to know? what have you Learned?) chart. They decided they wanted to know the following: "What's the difference between migration, immigration, and emigration?" and "Why did these people come to this country rather than go to some other country?"

During the course of this part of the expedition, we talked at length about the differences among migrants, immigrants, and emigrants. Whenever one of my children took a family trip during the course of the school year, we would talk about his or her "migration." I asked those students to keep journals and share them with the class on their return. Also, immigrants from the Atlanta area came to class to talk to us, including one parent from Jamaica; we prepared foods characteristic of various ethnic groups that have immigrated to the United States; and we created an Ellis Island drama simulation.

Based on a list of countries with the largest number of immigrants to the United States during the nineteenth century, my students chose the three countries they would most want to learn about and also gave me three names of classmates they would want to work with. I grouped them according to abilities and personalities, and assigned each of the seven groups a country, trying to give the children one of their choices.

Our final presentation of this learning expedition involved researching each country as a group, and writing a skit that incorporated all the answers to the following questions about the immigrant or migrant group: "Why did they come?" "Where did they come from, specifically?" "What kinds of hardships did they experience on the way?" "How did they travel here?" and "What hardships did they experience once they arrived?" This meant a lot more time spent in the library studying the history of these countries, reading plays and scripts, and again back in the classroom reading books above the fourth-grade level aloud to the class. Sometimes I would help the students group by group with the difficult books or articles by reading to them and helping them take notes. I used breaks from research in this period to teach the children theater techniques I had learned at the Civil Rights Summit from leaders Kim Archung and Kathy Greeley, such as voice theater and five sense poems (a poem reacting to something learned or experienced using the five senses).

Early on, one group told the class they were through. Although they said they had written their skit, they did not have a script. I did not say anything. We all went to the auditorium and watched them perform. Their peers knew that they had to give a positive critique first, and then ask questions. I sat silently while my students critiqued them to the point where they realized that their skit did not fit the students' criteria for the final presentation of their skits. The group realized there were so many questions that they could not answer that they had to revise the skit and write a script.

When the day of the final presentation arrived, all the groups were ready after many critique and revision sessions. I was amazed at how well my students were able to incorporate their research findings and theater tech-

niques into a commanding performance. I had tried play writing in the past without success, but this time I let my students make the decisions about how to present their work.

I was impressed with how much the children learned from each other. When one group decided to use a Five Sense Poem in its skit, others learned how powerfully those worked. They took the theater techniques I had taught them a step further: if the journey was long, they would say, "looooonnggg." Sometimes the students repeated words until they died out. Many of the groups held up signs for the other class members sitting in the audience instructing them to say words like *long* or *difficult* and the number of times to repeat them. During the performance, spontaneously, the audience got involved and felt a part of the skits.

The quality of the research also shone through the "fictitious" skits. For instance, we learned that people died along the journey to the United States. In one skit, a child died of an illness onboard a ship and had to be thrown overboard. They tossed this "person" off the stage wrapped in the British flag. In another skit, the children wrote about how Mexican immigrants were stopped by border police and sent back to Mexico. The immigrants then bought fake green cards that looked more realistic. At the end, they talked about the value of keeping their own language at home and how they would maintain their own culture.

If I were to repeat this expedition, I would focus on the African American experience beyond a discussion on black migration with the class. As an African American woman, I have found that to be a difficult subject for me to deal with personally. Because of the time in history I chose to stress, I touched only briefly on slavery.

I always share what I learn with my students, and I challenge them with my belief that if other students can do anything, *my* students can do it better. I felt they lived up to this expectation during this expedition.

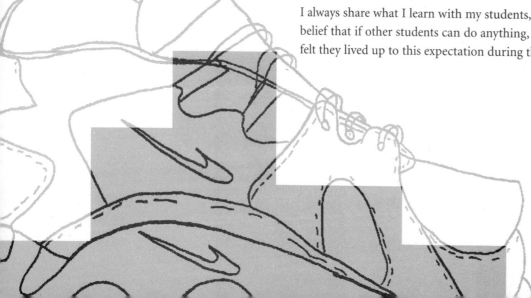

PLAN OUTLINE

TOPIC

Immigration/Migration

GUIDING QUESTIONS

~ Why do people, plants, and animals migrate?

~ What are migration and immigration?

~ What can we learn about some of the people, plants, and animals that migrate?

LEARNING GOALS

Knowledge and Content
Students will understand:

Science

~ The reasons that animals migrate; the anatomy and habitat of migrating animals

~ The connections between the migration patterns of people, plants, and animals

~ Seed production and plant classification; the reasons plants migrate

Social Studies

~ Reasons why people migrated and immigrated to the United States; issues of choice in the decision to migrate or immigrate

~ The major countries immigrant and migrant groups came from in the nineteenth century

~ Hardships immigrants and migrants encountered on their journeys and once they arrived in the country

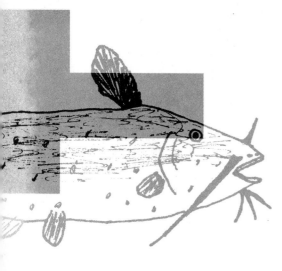

Language Arts

~ The skit and play as a genre of literature

~ Specific techniques used in theater; how to demonstrate performance skills

Art

~ The importance of quality craftsmanship; how to make an accurate representation of an animal

Skills and Habits
Students will practice and be able to:

~ use research, note-taking, and library and technology skills

~ write for and communicate to an audience the information they collect and read about animals, plants, and people

~ critique and revise until they attain a high level of quality

Character and Community
Students will practice and develop qualities of character and community, including:

~ an awareness of the difficulties involved in deciding whether or not to migrate or immigrate

~ the ability to work independently while keeping the goals of the group in mind

~ the ability to work collaboratively with small groups

PROJECTS

Project One
Each student selected an animal to research and created a drawing of the animal in its habitat, a sculpture of the animal using a unique sawdust medium, and wrote a report on the animal.

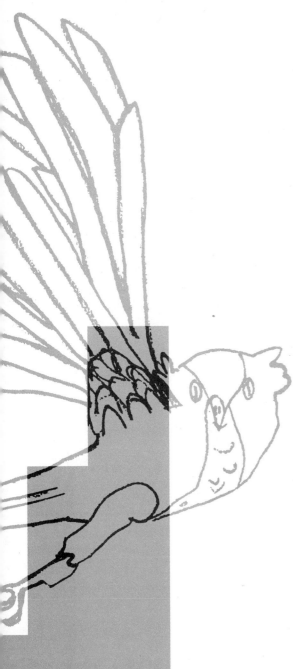

Learning Goals Addressed by the Project

Students learned research skills, focusing on the science content around animal migration, and turned the information into a written report. We focused on the editing and revision process, completing many drafts of the reports, and finally published them, using creative shapes and laminating them in "brochure" format. The art teacher taught the students to portray individual animals accurately. Each product stressed the importance of quality craftsmanship.

Ongoing Assessment

Students brainstormed a list of criteria to be used in a rubric for evaluation of the report. Students conducted peer critique of the various pieces of the project.

Project Two

As part of a final performance, students researched and collaboratively wrote a skit incorporating theater techniques, based on research on one country's immigration and migration patterns during the nineteenth century. The skits described why immigrants came from Ireland, Germany, Canada, the United Kingdom, Italy, Mexico, and the Soviet Union.

Learning Goals Addressed by the Project

This group project incorporated many of the learning goals mentioned earlier. Most important, students took information found during the research process, as well as theater skills taught in class, and transformed them into gripping skits presented to an audience at the school.

Major Activities/Steps

Students did research on immigration and migration of people from their assigned country, interviewed immigrants from various countries, and learned theater techniques. They brainstormed ideas for the script and began writing and practicing their productions. After each peer critique session, they revised the script and then performed it before an audience.

Goals of Activities/Steps

Students demonstrated their understanding of why immigrants came to the United States and the hardships experienced. In each skit, students incorporated two or three of the theater techniques taught during the course of the

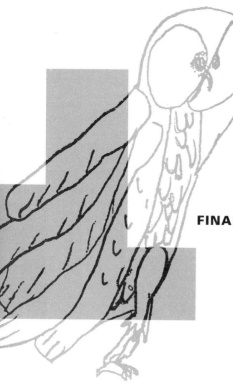

expedition, demonstrated the ability to work collaboratively with small groups, and effectively presented their writing to an audience.

Ongoing Assessment

We created rubric criteria for written skits, which I used in my evaluations of each team; students evaluated each other using the peer critique format. In addition, I evaluated them on the same rubric criteria daily or weekly on how well they worked as a group, used their time, helped each other with their work, and so forth.

FINAL ASSESSMENT

Students performed their skits in groups before an audience in the auditorium. After the performance, the audience wrote comments about the skits in a log book. The class members then led the audience back to the classroom where students sat at their desks and presented their animal reports, sculptures, and drawings, and answered questions from visitors. Murals depicting the life of the seed were displayed on the walls around the room. I used a rubric created with the students to evaluate them. I also based my evaluation on how well the audience perceived and understood their work.

RESOURCES

Books

Lord, Bette Bao. *In the Year of the Boar and Jackie Robinson.* New York: Harper and Row, 1986. (Read aloud.)

Mohr, Nicolasa. *Felita.* New York: Bantam, 1990.

In addition to these class readings, the students read many other books related to their research.

Experts

Students interviewed immigrants who visited the class to describe their own experiences with immigrating or migrating to this country.

Fieldwork Sites

Students visited Emory University's presentation of "Souls Grown Deep," an art exhibit of African American folk art from the Southeast. This served as an early kickoff for the people section of the expedition, as well as inspiration for the sculpture project.

Students visited the Jimmy Carter Library to view immigration stories through photographs. Students did a scavenger hunt to answer questions about conditions people experienced during their traveling, as well as hardships experienced once they were living in the United States.

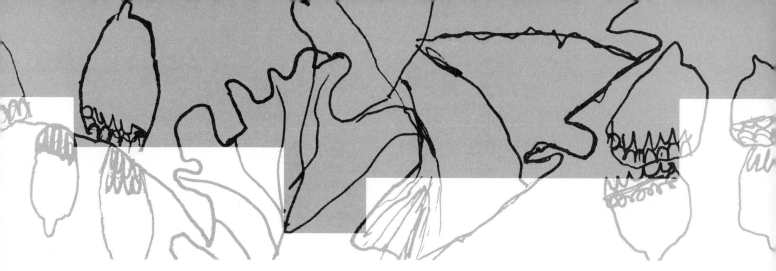

A Sixth-Grade Learning Expedition
on Ecology and Service

CHERYL SIMS
School for the Physical City
New York, New York

I wanted to find a way to bring the subject of ecology to life for my two sixth-grade Life Science classes, and to provide an active learning experience that would motivate them to learn. I also wanted to create a learning experience that would foster an ethic of service, a desire to use what the students learned about ecology to do something of value for their community. So I decided to integrate service learning into the study of ecology in the learning expedition "How Humans Impact the Natural World."

I thought that students would be more engaged and would learn science more deeply in the context of the community, and that is what happened. Students learned more about the core concepts and tools of ecology because they were using what they had learned to make a real contribution to their school neighborhood. Service learning was tied clearly to academics, so students could see how their academic learning could benefit their community and the environment. I asked the students to identify a need in the community related to their studies, to plan and organize an event that would address that need, and to assess the progress of their work. Within these parameters, it was left up to the students to decide what the project would be, and how they would organize it.

I developed learning goals for content, learning skills, habits of mind, and character related to three different standards.

New York City's *Essential Learning Outcomes* for Life Science

Students learned core knowledge and concepts of ecology such as species interactions, how the actions of humans impact not only their survival in the environment but also affect other species (plants and animals); soil composition and the characteristics necessary to make soil acceptable for vegetation; microorganisms and how soil is made through the process of decomposition; and the flow of matter in a community—the ways in which organic matter decomposes and is recycled to produce new life.

Performance standards for applied learning from *New Standards* (National Center on Education and the Economy and the University of Pittsburgh), which have been adopted by the school's district

Students planned and organized an applied learning service project related to their academic studies and developed a game plan, based on what they learned conducting a needs assessment, to restore park vegetation. Students also organized themselves into groups and reflected on their progress in journals.

Expeditionary Learning Outward Bound Design Principles

Responsibility for Learning
Students took significant responsibility for directing their own personal and collective learning by designing,

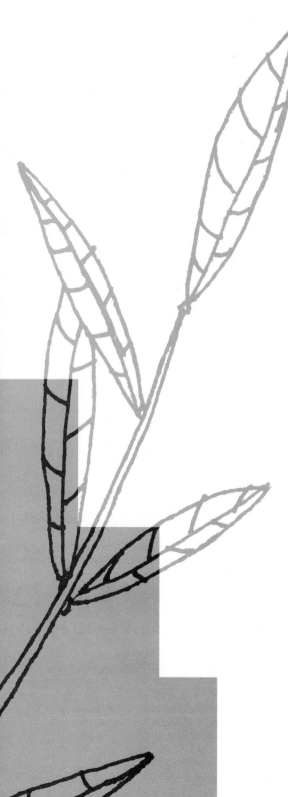

planning, and carrying out the Madison Park ecology-based service learning project. Students contacted outside experts, decided on the steps needed to accomplish their goals, and determined what information to include in their final presentation.

The Natural World

Students developed a direct and respectful relationship with the natural world, learned important lessons about the recurring cycles of cause and effect, and learned to become stewards of the earth as they applied their academic studies of ecology to restore the natural habitat of Madison Park.

Service and Compassion

Students developed a strong ethic of service and compassion as they reflected on the meaning of service, agreed on a shared definition of what service meant to them, and used their time, talents, and knowledge to serve others.

With these goals in mind, I assessed the success of the learning expedition using questions such as these: Did students gain an in-depth understanding of the most important core concepts, thinking approaches, and tools of ecology? Did they use what they learned to address real-life problems in the way that professionals would? Did they become better thinkers and problem-solvers as they worked together to plan and carry out their service project? Were they motivated to put their learning to the service of their community? Could they share their learning with others and communicate what they had learned effectively using multiple forms of media?

Students documented their work and progress by producing a video that documented their service project; creating a HyperStudio stack (a multimedia software tool that lets students create a set of "cards" on the computer to organize and present their ideas) that demonstrated what they had learned; and making an oral presentation of their work to an outside audience.

LAYING THE GROUNDWORK

In addition to studying in the classroom the key principles and concepts of ecology, such as forest layers, compaction, and decomposition, I had students engage in several activities to prepare them to plan and implement their project. They did surveys of parks, polled people who use the parks, compiled statistics of organisms that depend on the parks, and surveyed people's environmental concerns. Students conducted several different kinds of research, including searching the Internet, reading books about New York City and plant ecology, watching videos, and making telephone calls to obtain information about agencies that help the environment.

We contacted experts such as the Urban Park Rangers and the Department of Environmental Conservation (DEC). Both organizations participated in a panel discussion with the students on environmental issues in general and on their roles in serving the environment. They also gave us leads on places we could investigate for different service projects.

We took a tour of Inwood Park so that students could learn more about the ecology of a forest and relate what they learned there to the ecology of local parks in their community. After preparing students with the help of an Inwood Park curriculum guide, we visited the park a second time to help with reforestation. The rangers talked with the students about the importance of this service activity. We also went to the Lower East Side Ecology Center, a grassroots recycling and composting effort, where the students learned about recycling, worm bins, and microorganisms that help to enrich the soil and break down organic materials.

MADISON SQUARE PARK SERVICE PROJECT

After the students gathered and analyzed all the information from these activities and from the contacts they had made, they chose Madison Square Park as the ideal place for their service project. They decided they could realistically do park restoration. They contacted the superintendent of the Parks Department and made arrangements to work in the park each week to help undo some of the damage to the lawns that young people had created by playing on them. As part of the restoration project, students reseeded and watered lawns, planted flowers, picked up litter, and mulched the grounds.

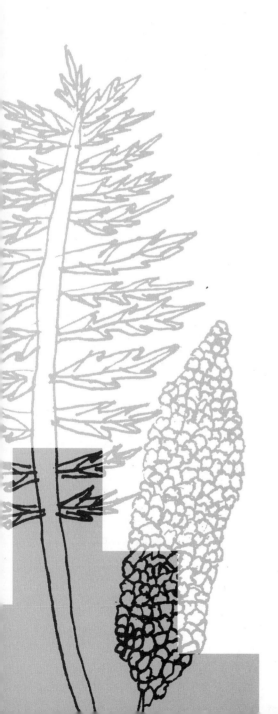

Before beginning the restoration, students went into the park and mapped out an area where they would make observations and survey the damage. Using what they had learned about ecological concepts, the students surveyed the park for human and animal use, and took an inventory of plant and animal species. They did a neighborhood walk to look at local gardens and parks, and made inquiries in plant stores about the best types of plants to grow in partly shaded areas. Students marked off quadrants that they would investigate in depth, where they took notes on soil erosion and dryness, estimated how much oxygen could be produced by the trees and shrubs of the area they mapped, and took measurements of the depth of soil compaction. From these observations students planned, with the help of park personnel, where strategically to place plants and grass seeds. Students created a needs assessment and restoration plan by using the same tools and approaches that professionals use in real life, and held themselves to real-life standards. Did their restoration project actually restore the natural habitat of the park in a lasting way?

As they were adding the finishing touches to the park, a neighborhood elementary school asked the students to host a third-grade class at the park. The students organized themselves into five groups. Each group created a station for the third graders to visit. They taught the youngsters about planting flowers and about the anatomy of a flower; they also held a contest for picking up litter in the park and did a skit on why people should not litter. Students decided on and did fund-raising to pay for the flowers they used in their work with the third graders. The last station taught the younger students about environmental issues such as pollution and recycling. After the lesson, students played a game with the youngsters to assess their retention of the information.

For a culminating celebration, students presented their work to an audience of parents, faculty, and school friends. Students read from journals, shared poems, showed a video, hung posters and pictures in gallery fashion, and displayed letters from third graders in response to their day at the park. They also walked guests through the information in their HyperStudio stack. One student served as master of ceremonies, while others took turns doing these activities. Students really demonstrated what they valued most from the expedition during the question-and-answer period held at the end of the celebration. I could see their excitement as many students raised their hands to field questions from the audience.

LEARNING RESULTS

As I looked at student learning and the quality of work that students produced during the expedition, I saw a real value to ecology and service as integrated themes. Each focus seemed to support and build upon the other.

Students learned the science curriculum more deeply because they knew that they would have to apply what they learned to do something that had become important to them. I saw improvement in students' language skills by the end of the expedition, as they used ecological terms in describing the necessity of their service work. They had a greater understanding of the impact that humans can have on the natural environment, and what humans can do to restore and sustain natural habitats that they have damaged.

I also saw evidence that students developed a stronger ethic of service, and that the opportunity to be of service engaged students in learning. Students who already had a sense of community and responsibility toward the environment had their values reinforced by the project; and those students who were indifferent toward the environment had their consciousness raised about how their actions affect the environment. One boy who frequently did not turn in assignments kept his journal current and asked repeatedly when we would go to the park to do more work. I was excited to see my students working in the park during their lunch period in small groups without any prompting from the park personnel or me. Students expressed feelings of ownership of the park, looked at it as more than a place to play, and took on responsibility to maintain it. They would get upset whenever some older students played on the lawn or an adult walked through a flower bed.

I was particularly proud of the way the students embraced the opportunity to help younger students learn what they had learned. While they were working with the third graders, I saw my class replicate some of the activities I had done with them. For instance, I taught them how to do a flower dissection so that they could get a sense of the components of plant reproduction. My students, in turn, did the same exercise with the youngsters using flowers they had purchased, literature from a science text, and a chart they had designed on poster board. This showed me that students had both developed an ethic of service and really learned about ecology.

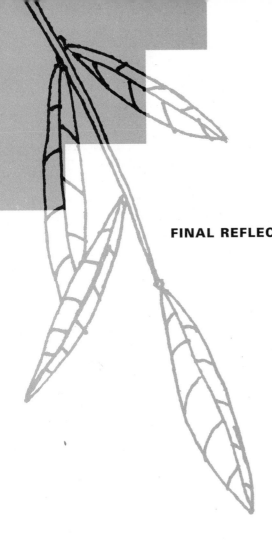

The students also learned how to work well together and coordinate their work to get the project done. Although two classes worked on the project and rarely shared a class period together, this did not pose a problem for them in sharing ideas. They collaborated through the computer or at play during lunch.

FINAL REFLECTIONS

If I were to do it again, I would probably structure the expedition so that it would involve more of the writing process, and I would add activities related more to the environmental science curriculum—including soil testing and having students develop models of the layers of soil representing organisms found in soil during the recycling process of composting. This would help inform their decisions about how to restore and maintain the environment.

More practice with the video cameras and editing machines would have enhanced the quality of documentation. A handset and headphones would have allowed students to improve the sound quality of their videotapes.

I also would have concentrated on the assessment process more. I relied heavily on observation and discussion for evaluating the project. Although my students and I had an idea of what a successful project would look like, there was nothing written to set criteria for how we would get to the place we wanted to go. In the future I would have students design a rubric that they would use to monitor their progress to go along with observations and class discussions. I would also have students keep a portfolio illustrating the applied learning standards, science objectives, and rubrics they were working toward.

Overall, I think students realized that they should be concerned about their environment and that they could do something to protect it. My observations of how students respond to environmental issues that come up in other classes have been the biggest measure of the expedition's lasting impact. Recently, in a math class I had this opportunity. A group of thirteen-year-olds who had participated in this expedition last year was given the following math problem: "A school asked its science club to figure out which type of camera would be the best buy for taking yearbook pictures." The problem went on to give specific information about the cost of disposable cameras and of regular 35-mm cameras. The information provided by the problem also included how many pictures each camera could take, as well as the cost of film development.

While all the other students spent time calculating that the disposable cameras were cheaper and that, therefore, the school should buy them, the students who had participated in the ecology expedition drew a different conclusion. Their reasoning for why the school should buy the 35-mm cameras, which also shows me their ability to think critically, was simple: "Although the disposable ones were cheaper, it would be more economical and environmentally friendly to purchase the 35-mms. This is because the regular cameras can be reused for taking yearbook photos in the future, while disposable cameras can only be used once and add to the solid waste problem."

In this expedition students will learn what constitutes a community, how populations are defined, what interspecies relationships exist within a community, and how humans and their resources have affected other species in both negative and positive ways. Finally, students will learn how to be proactive in making positive contributions to their environment.

TOPIC

How Humans Impact the Natural World

GUIDING QUESTIONS

~ What are some ways humans interact with the natural world?

~ Which human interactions with the natural environment are positive and which are negative?

~ What are the implications of these interactions for our future?

~ What can we do to reduce the negative effects of human interactions in the natural environment?

LEARNING GOALS

Knowledge and Content
Students will understand:

~ core ecological concepts, such as compaction, erosion, population, and community

~ the interrelationship between organisms and their environment, and recurring cycles of cause and effect in the natural world

~ the fact that humans can sometimes disrupt the balance of nature by altering natural communities

~ various uses of forests and parklands for the preservation of wildlife, soil and water conservation, and recreation

Skills and Habits
Students will:

~ practice gathering data, assimilating prior knowledge, and problem solving to put their new knowledge to use where others might benefit

~ learn to document their work through more than one medium, such as computers, video, and journals

~ make measurements, interpret data, and convey their findings

~ carry out research using multiple methods and media

Character and Community
Students will:

~ develop a respect for the environment and exercise habits that demonstrate that respect

~ understand that individuals and society have a responsibility to maintain the quality of the natural world

PROJECTS

Madison Square Park Service Project
This project is designed to help students realize that they can play an active role in making changes to their environment. Students will be asked to identify a need in a community relating to their studies, to plan and organize an event that will address that need, and to evaluate the progress of their work.

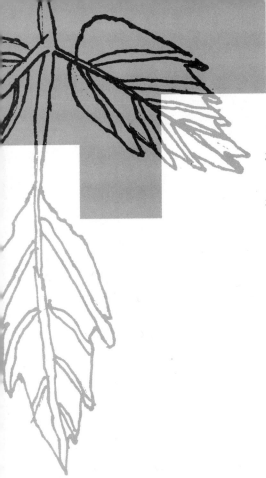

The documentation of their progress will take place in three ways:

1. Video will be used to document their service work

2. A HyperStudio stack will be created to demonstrate what students are learning

3. An oral presentation of completed work will be made to an outside audience

The exact form of video, computer program, and oral presentation will be determined by the students. However, they will all have to include use of ecological or environmental terms, demonstrate clearly an understanding of what constitutes service, and show evidence that a service is being provided that impacts the environment in a positive way.

Activities and Tasks

Activities that relate to service

Introduce students to the concept of service, and elicit from students the definition of service through several initiatives.

Service Initiative One

The teacher "trashes" the classroom before students arrive. While other initiatives are going on, the teacher observes the behavior students show toward the trash. When the other initiatives have been completed, the teacher initiates a discussion about the trash, and the whole class reflects on how service could have been, or was done in regards to the trash.

Service Initiative Two

Students are given a list of actions people might engage in. They are to determine whether they think the actions constitute service or not. After discussing their decision in small groups, the students are to take turns reporting to the whole group how they arrived at their decision. For example, they might be asked if it is a service if someone organizes a community project to fix up abandoned buildings and then writes to local newspapers about it.

Service Initiative Three

Students are handed a piece of paper with a description of a service they can perform for someone. For instance, the paper might say "unload a person's burden," or "make someone smile." With the task in mind, students are to seek out people as they go through the school day for whom they could per-

form the action with which they were challenged. Afterward they are to reflect on what happened and how they felt, emotionally as well as intellectually.

Service Initiative Four
Students are given journals in which to record service work and their thoughts on services performed. Students are asked to log in their journals interviews of family members regarding their experience with service.

Activities to develop, plan, and carry out the project
Project Activity One
Students research frequently discussed environmental concerns using the Internet and books. Then they construct a survey to poll the public about the concerns. Specific goals are to graph the results of the poll and determine which needs the students can address.

Project Activity Two
Students make contact with outside agencies to gain information about supplies, tools, permits, and so forth, that they may need to conduct their service work. They make a budget for supplies they will need.

Project Activity Three
Students divide up the workload for the project based on the resources available, site limitations, and the demands of the project.

Project Activity Four
Students implement the service plan and document the progress of what they learn from it by using their journals, photographs, videos, and HyperStudio card stacks. The entries should reflect the connections between their service work and the ecology concepts they have studied. For example, students should be able to explain the ecological significance of planting trees on a ridge, and they should know and be able to explain exactly how their actions help the environment.

Project Activity Five
Students present the results of their work to an outside audience through graphic, oral, and written displays.

Activities related to ecology that go on concurrently with service practices

Students will use resources such as teacher handouts, class notes, and reading materials from both books and the Internet, videotapes, and walking tours of parks and gardens to help them accomplish the following tasks:

~ Explain the different roles of the various layers of the forest

~ Estimate the amount of oxygen produced for a designated area

~ Identify all parts of a flower and state their functions with regard to reproduction

~ Mark a one-square-meter quadrant and describe the ecological conditions of that area, including noting whether any evidence exists to suggest damage or litter by humans

~ View several tapes on environmental issues from the Educational Video Center library, and discuss how those issues relate to their service project

~ Gather information from the Lower East Side Ecology center and use the language of science to describe the natural process of the earth's recycling system

~ Use information from the New York Historical Society and the book *New York Walking Tours* to determine the impact of urban progress on parklands

Multimedia activities

A consultant from Educational Video Center will explain the procedures for shooting and editing a video. Students will:

~ walk through a checklist of priorities when handling a camera to obtain the best shots

~ have time to practice camera techniques before they actually shoot footage for their video

~ watch a demonstration of a HyperStudio program and be given guidelines on how to produce their own card stack to document their work

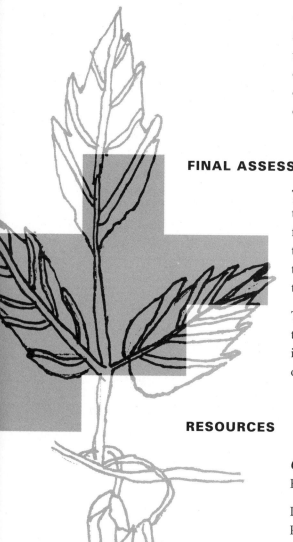

Ongoing Assessment

Students are to look at models of existing service projects to determine their own focus. The students' progress in the project and their understanding of the science concepts embedded in the project will be determined by ongoing discussions, written reflections in journals, and communications of understanding made through HyperStudio card stacks and video.

FINAL ASSESSMENT

The results of the students' work (whether they did indeed do something to change a negative effect of human ecology), large group discussions, the final presentations of their project, and their journal reflections (whether there is evidence that they have changed their own habits or attitudes toward the natural world) will determine the success of the students and their project.

The assessment will be accomplished by setting standards for presentations that include quality of oral communications, evidence of science concepts in speeches and written text relating to the environment, and observations of students' actions both in and out of class.

RESOURCES

Organizations and Institutions

Educational Video Center library and personnel

Local and national environmental organizations such as Environmental Protection Agency, Green Guerrillas, Operation Green Thumb

City and state agencies: New York City Parks Department, Department of Environmental Protection, Department of Environmental Conservation, Urban Planning office, Urban Park Rangers

Institutions, museums, and parks: New York Historical Society; American Museum of Natural History; Central Park Conservancy and Dairy Botanical Gardens; Wave Hill; Lower East Side Ecology Center; neighborhood parks and gardens, including those in the Lower East Side

New York City Outward Bound Center

Various websites with environmental material, local libraries

Videos

Educational Video Center: *Trash Thy Neighbor; New York City and The Hudson River: Downstream and Up a Creek; City Nature*

Department of Environmental Protection: *Dripnet*

Reading Material

Burnie, David. *Dictionary of Nature.* New York: Dorling Kindersley, 1994.

City Green, newsletter of Brooklyn Center for the Urban Environment

The EarthWorks Group. *50 Simple Things Kids Can Do to Save the Earth.* Kansas City, Mo.: Andrews and McMeel, 1990.

"The Environment Can Take Care of Itself," essay by Andrew Chrisomalis of River Dell Junior High School, River Edge, N. J.

Ganeri, Anita. *What's Inside Plants?* New York: Peter Bedrick Books, 1995.

Life science textbooks

News articles from various New York City newspapers

Perry, Frances, ed. *Guide to Plants and Flowers.* New York: Simon and Schuster, 1974.

Serim, Ferdi. *NetLearning: Why Teachers Use the Internet.* Songline Studios, 1996.

Solid Waste: Is There a Solution? New York Science Technology and Society booklet.

Teacher's Guide: Bringing the Classroom into the Forest. Reference material from Inwood Park.

Wolfe, Gerard R. *New York Guide to the Metropolis: New York Walking Tours of Architecture and History.* McGraw-Hill, Inc.

YO TV Handbook for making videos, from the Educational Video Center

Books! Books! Books!
A First-Grade Expedition into Becoming Readers and Writers

NORA GILL
Table Mound Elementary School
Dubuque, Iowa

For the student beginning first grade, literacy skills become the major instructional focus. This twelve-week expedition, "Books! Books! Books!," immerses students in literature and the skills of reading, writing, listening, and speaking in a way that helps them become engaged and motivated learners.

First graders start the school year by embarking on a journey to become readers and writers. By the end of the expedition, students have become beginning readers who have read as many as fifty books with and to their parents, and budding authors and playwrights who have written individual and class books, and created and performed a class play. Along the way, students learn and practice essential literacy skills in a context that gives them a reason to learn, using their new skills to work on projects that have meaning for them.

The process of learning to read and write cannot be left to chance. Students need to learn specific skills and strategies to go to the next steps. Since every child learns to read in a different way and at a different pace, the challenge

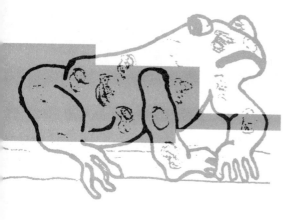

of teaching becomes one of assessing where each student is along the continuum. The teacher uses instructional practices that will move each child along the road to becoming a fluent reader and writer.

"Books! Books! Books!" is designed with clear learning goals that are based on the curricular expectations for first grade and are reflective of the reading/language arts standards adopted by the district. Learning expeditions are frequently based on a topic in science or social studies. Teaching an expedition centered around a theme is difficult at the beginning of first grade because classrooms usually have limited sets of books at a developmentally appropriate reading level to support a specific topic. Through its focus on becoming readers and writers, "Books! Books! Books!" allows the use of a wider selection of existing or available sets of books, big books, and stories.

Through minor projects, students build a foundation of the content, skills, and habits they will need for the major class projects: writing two class books, and creating and performing a Thanksgiving class play. The play, which the class decided to create for Thanksgiving, was not originally planned as a major project. From the children's point of view, however, it became the expedition's culminating project. Creating a play they were proud of gave students a reason to become better readers and writers.

There is ongoing assessment throughout the expedition. An initial assessment is made of each child at the beginning of the expedition and again at the end of the first trimester. As early as the second week students began to use reflection, critique, and revision in their writing, using peer and teacher critique to do multiple drafts before producing their final "best" draft. Every time students get ready to write or do artwork, they start by singing this chant:

> *Good, better, best*
> *I will always do my best*
> *to make my good better*
> *and my better my best.*

Building a classroom community and learning and practicing collaboration is a regular focus from the very beginning to create a positive learning environment.

"Books! Books! Books!" is designed to create a learning environment and experience from the very first day of first grade which would achieve several of the school district's language arts outcomes:

- Promotes an engagement and appreciation of literature supported by a home-school connection

- Fosters a positive attitude and integrates the skills of reading, writing, listening, and speaking

- Provides immersion in a print-rich, stimulating learning environment for students that encourages risk taking and exploration

WHAT WE DID AND HOW WE DID IT

Correspondence with Parents

Throughout the expedition, in what could be thought of as an ongoing family project, students read with and to their parents at home, including the books that they have written at school. Months after the end of the expedition, students are still checking out the books and taking them home to share with their parents. Each month a newsletter goes home to parents explaining the progress of the expedition and the learning of the students. This also provides an opportunity to communicate to parents information on how they need to be active partners in educating their children. It is important for parents to read to their children, ask about school, and allow their children to read to them, sharing the joy and excitement of early learning.

How Do You Fit It All In

As you read the district's grade-level expectations, there are multiple responsibilities teachers have that may not fit nicely into the topic of the current learning expedition. For example, the science expectations include knowledge of weather, weather conditions, and how those affect decisions on what to wear. Each morning, during the opening circle, information on the weather is recorded, including the temperature—a math concept. The point is that teachers have a multitude of instructional responsibilities that must be included in the flow of the day. However, if the instruction and interaction with students are based on the ten design principles of Expeditionary Learning, it is truly an Expeditionary Learning classroom.

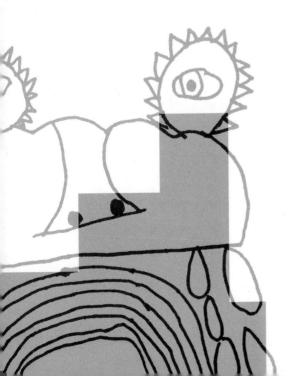

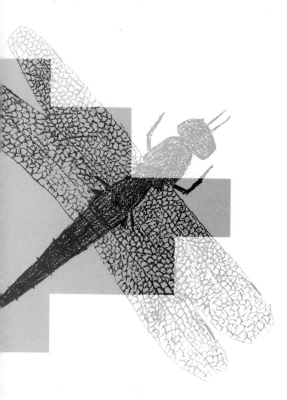

Beginning a New Year: A Typical Day

For an Expeditionary Learning teacher, building community within the group becomes the first responsibility. During the first few weeks of community circle, name games and "ice breaker" initiatives allow the students to get to know one another and establish a safe and caring environment for the students.

A typical day in the classroom usually begins with an opening community circle and the tasks of attendance, pledge, lunch count, calendar, and weather. Following the opening circle, students participate in journal writing. Since most students begin the first grade with very limited writing skills, ideas for the journal writing are discussed (such as pets, family, friends, places they have been, and things they like to do).

Students then return to their tables and draw a picture of what they want to write about. They are encouraged to write one short sentence about the picture. Students frequently respond that they do not know how to write or spell. This is the point for the teacher to teach the skill of stretching out the sounds of the words and trying to identify the sounds, even if it is only a beginning sound. Spiral notebook journals are used every day, for the whole group, during the first few weeks. The journal writing becomes a center activity after the first few weeks.

An individual "ABC" book is one of the minor projects the students then work on. First we sing the "ABC" song, and the teacher then reads aloud an ABC book, followed by having the students say the "ABCs" using flashcards with both upper- and lower-case letters. Beginning with the consonants, students might brainstorm things that start with B. The teacher would then list the items on a piece of chart paper. Using a picture file (pictures cut from magazines) students would choose an item from the file that begins with that consonant, and be able to identify the item. Students then paste the picture on the appropriate page of their own ABC book. The books are pre-made—1/4 sheets of paper, comb bound. The letters are lightly penciled in on the corner of each page. Each student traces over the letter, and the teacher circulates and writes the name of the item under the pasted picture.

Each day students are expected to reread the pages of the book with a partner. This is an excellent review of letters and beginning sounds.

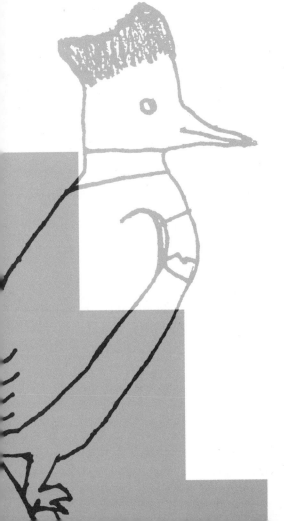

After a snack and a fifteen-minute recess, math instruction follows—usually for about forty minutes—taking the class up to lunchtime.

In the afternoon, we begin with show and tell. There are five tables of students in the class, so each table is able to participate once a week.

The students then gather on the carpet for a "read aloud" story time. The first three weeks focus on Dr. Seuss books, followed by other authors. Students are encouraged to bring in other books by the featured author, videotapes, and toys.

During the first two weeks the students work on a color book. A color book is read to the students, followed by the students brainstorming items of the color described. The suggested items are recorded on chart paper, with the teacher sketching a simple picture of the item next to the word. After the students return to their seats, the teacher models a sentence pattern using the color word, such as "I like red." Students copy the sentence while the teacher instructs the skills/strategies of finger space between words, letter formation, beginning sentences with capital letters, letter recognition, letter sounds, and periods. This is modeled and practiced immediately.

Each day the students create a separate color book, made from four 1/4 sheets. The cover of each book is cut from construction paper of the color the students are studying. On each page the students have to write the sentence and then draw a picture of some item of that color. Students complete as many pages of the book as time allows.

Students take the color books home each night and read to their parents, bringing the books back the next day and placing them in their individual book boxes in the classroom. Students complete eight colors, the project culminating in their creation of a color review book, including a page for each color, with the sentence pattern and student-created drawings.

Most afternoons end with specialist time: art, music, and physical education. When possible, the specialists craft their own lessons around the stories being read in the classroom.

Each day often ends with a quick check-in with students—reviewing what was learned that day, and checking that they have the color book and a classroom library book packed to go home. Students are to read the color books to their parents, and parents are to read the classroom library books to the students. A tally sheet of books read by parents to students is kept, with many parents reading more than fifty different books from the classroom library to their children by the end of the expedition.

Weeks One and Two

As a kickoff activity, the school's principal arrives in class dressed for a part in *Little Red Riding Hood* and performs a dramatic reading of the story. This also begins a series of guest readers invited to spend time reading aloud their favorite or a teacher-selected children's book. Resources for the guest readers include parents, grandparents, school/business partners, community members, students from the drama departments of area colleges, and community theater members. Students produce thank-you notes on the computer (using any card-making program). This, of course, means instructional time on the use of the computer.

The projects students work on during the first two weeks include the ABC books and the color books. Instruction in reading and writing skills and strategies is infused into the authentic work the students are creating. The use of teacher-prepared worksheets is kept to a minimum. Students are encouraged to bring favorite stories/books to class. Students share their books with a small group or partner and with the class in read-aloud sessions.

During the second week, learning centers are set up around the room. This allows the teacher to have time with small groups or individual students to assess their reading and writing. Centers are introduced one at a time so that students receive instruction and directions about the purpose and use of each center. For the first few days, the teacher circulates and assists students with instructions and purposes. Only after students understand and show appropriate use of the centers does the teacher begin working with individual students on assessment.

The initial assessments include the recognition and writing of upper- and lower-case letters, beginning consonant sounds, basic sight word recognition, sentence dictation, and a running record of leveled reading books. This information is used to create five homogeneous reading and writing instructional groups.

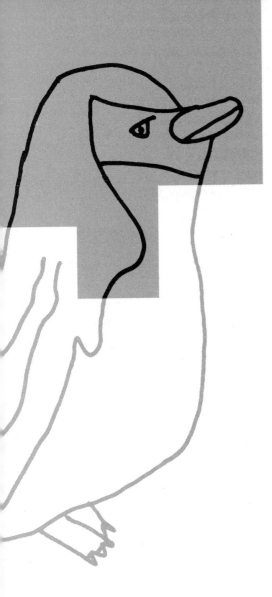

Weeks Two, Three, and Four

The daily lessons continue with a similar schedule. The color books are completed by the end of the second week. Work on the ABC books continues. Center ideas change as the students' skills improve, with some centers focusing on instructional issues of math, computer usage, art, and science, in addition to the centers that focus on reading and writing.

Shared reading with the teacher follows the district's Macmillan reading program, including a big book by Anthony Browne entitled *I Like Books*. This sets the stage for the student product—a student-produced book about different kinds of books or what books are about. We begin with a KWL (what do you Know? what do you Want to know? and what have you Learned?) brainstorm session on what books are about. Each page of the student book includes a teacher-prompt that is on the overhead. Students then draw a picture on the page that illustrates the answer to the teacher-prompt. Students are expected to create a rough draft, complete a peer critique of the page, do revisions, then a teacher critique, another revision, and then the final "best" draft. The final product includes a title page and four response pages. Books are shared daily with partner pairs and small groups and are also shared with a sixth-grade "buddy" who comes into the classroom once every two weeks. The final product is taken home, read to parents, and then returned to the classroom's individual student book box.

It is during this time that the class is introduced to the school library, and students learn how to check out books to take home for parents to read to them. Instruction in the use of the computer continues with student-produced products, including the thank-you notes to guest readers.

Weeks Five, Six, Seven, and Eight

The mornings during this time really focus on the centers, reading instruction in small groups, and math. Project time in the afternoon includes a variety of experiences, such as going to the public library, outlining the experience, and then dictating an experience story about the trip. The story is written on the overhead, and when it is completed, the teacher types it out on the computer. The pages are divided into sixteen parts, with each of sixteen students taking a page. One small group of six more-advanced students uses the computers in the library to create a computer-generated book on the trip to the public library. Each of the sixteen students is required to read and illustrate his or her page, using the same critique and

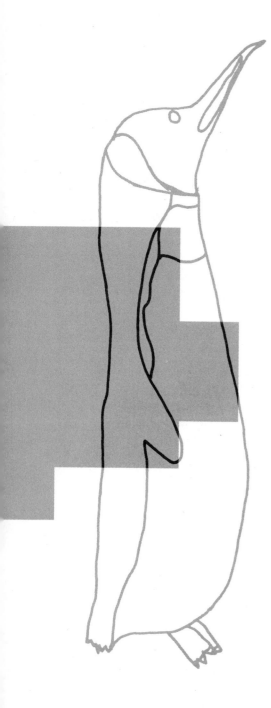

revision sequence. The final product on the class trip to the public library is laminated, comb bound, read many times in class, and is made available, with a card pocket placed in the back, for students to check out and take home to read to their parents.

With the ABC book, the vowels are introduced, including short vowel and long vowel sounds and words. The ABC center is set up to allow students to find pictures, write the word, and create a poster for each vowel sound.

Beginning with nursery rhymes, the teacher reads the selection, picking out certain vocabulary words and a phonics skill that students highlight on their copies. Each page includes space for original artwork by the students. Poetry follows the nursery rhymes—poems around a fall season theme.

Hardee's Restaurant, a business partner with the school, provides the class with white bags that the students use to create an illustration of their favorite book. The bag illustrations go through a series of activities: a first draft on separate paper, peer and self critique, revision, teacher critique and revision, and then final copy colored on the bag, including the name of the book, name of the author, student's name, and the name of the school. The bags are returned to Hardee's, where they are used for customers.

After the individual ABC books have been completed, the students are exposed to a great variety of ABC books, stories, and songs. As a culmination, the students decided to create a class ABC book based on different animals. As a class, the students brainstorm and select an animal for each letter of the alphabet. Students then select the animal they want to illustrate, and each student creates a page in the book. Five students are allowed to complete their first page and then choose a second so that all letters are completed. The illustrations, along with captions, go through the same critique and revision sequence prior to developing the final copy. The pages are laminated and bound, a pocket is placed in the back, and the book is checked out to be read to parents at home.

Weeks Nine, Ten, Eleven, and Twelve

The routine and culture of the class is set. When there are problems at lunch or on the playground, the community circle allows us the opportunity to discuss appropriate student behavior in a positive and safe manner. As a group we spend time discussing the differences between tattling and

informing, between put-downs and positive feedback. The students become good at expressing themselves by saying "I noticed…," or "We were…," or "Somebody…," rather than "He did…," or "She didn't…."

After reading the big book *Rain* by Robert Kalan, students follow the pattern of the story: "Rain on the…" (color and object—for example, rain on the red car). There are five different sentences using five different objects and colors. The only prompt is the introduction, "Rain on the…." Students design a title page, write, and illustrate each of the five pages with the same sequence of good, better, best drafts. At the end of the book, students draw a rainbow, following the design of the original book.

Instruction in the writing process continues with the introduction of descriptive writing and a descriptive paragraph. The teacher models the process by cutting out a picture and writing the three descriptive sentences. Students cut a picture from a magazine and write a descriptive paragraph of three or more sentences about the picture. This rough draft is saved by the teacher, stamped with "rough draft," as an example of the early writing attempt. A second picture is chosen, and again, the writing process includes a rough draft, checking to see if it makes sense (revision), checking for spelling and punctuation (editing), and using self and peer critique. There is a classroom rule stating that a student must check with three others prior to asking the teacher. The final product is placed in the writing portfolio as an example of quality work.

For Thanksgiving, the class decided to create a class play or pageant about the Pilgrims coming to America. Class time is spent exposing the students to a variety of stories, books, and a video on the Pilgrims and Thanksgiving. Students retell the story orally. The story is divided into five parts, one for each table of students (heterogeneous groups). Each student identifies a character he or she would represent, creates a script, and checks to see if each part makes sense when put together; then students make props to go with their lines. Students practice the play, have a dress rehearsal, and put on the play for the other two first-grade classes and the two kindergarten classes. The actual play was videotaped by a couple of sixth-grade students, and a copy of the play was then made available for students to take home. This became the culminating project for the expedition.

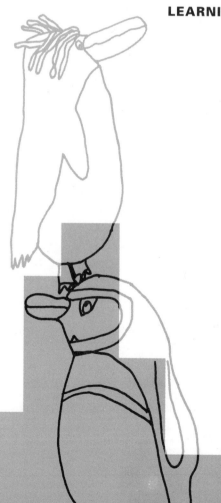

PLAN OUTLINE

TOPIC

Reading and Writing

GUIDING QUESTIONS

～ How will I learn how to read and write?

～ What do good readers and writers do?

～ How do you find the kind of book you want in a library?

～ How do authors get ideas and write a story?

LEARNING GOALS

To know

～ Several authors of children's books

～ How to read and spell color words

～ Basic sight vocabulary

～ Beginning, ending, and middle consonant sounds

～ How to use *strategies* to read

～ How to recognize the numerals and their values from zero to twenty

～ Nursery rhymes, and other poems about friendship and fall

～ How to find and check out a book

～ The steps of process writing

～ How to write a descriptive paragraph

～ How to make a class big book story

～ Different genres of books

～ The difference between an author and an illustrator

～ How to use technology for reading and writing

～ How to write and perform a play

～ How to make friends and be a friend

To do

- Listen to and enjoy stories by selected authors and in selected genres
- Read and recite favorite poems in poetry notebook
- Make a color book on each color
- Make an individual ABC book
- Participate in guided reading discussions and read leveled books
- Make two number books (0–12, 13–20)
- Go to the school library and check out books
- Check out books daily from the classroom library

- Record books read at home on Home Reading sheet
- Participate in making a class big book about going to the city library
- Write in journals daily
- Write a descriptive paragraph using the processes of writing
- Work quietly and cooperatively in centers
- Read books during D.E.A.R. time (Drop Everything and Read)
- Use the classroom computers
- Bring a favorite book from home and share with class

To be

- Good listeners, able to enjoy stories
- Authors and illustrators of original work
- Readers and writers

- Contributors to group work
- Users of the library
- Users of age-appropriate technology
- Cooperative learners and workers
- A friend

MINOR PROJECTS

- Make color books
- Make an individual ABC book
- Start a poetry notebook (continue all year)
- Make two number books
- Decorate bags from school business partners with picture of favorite book

- Write thank-you notes to guest readers
- Make an individual book called *I Like Books*
- Publish a descriptive paragraph

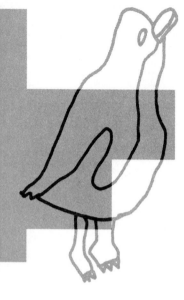

MAJOR PROJECTS

~ Make a class big book—an ABC book

~ Make a class big book about going to the city library

~ Put on a class play

~ Start an ongoing family home reading project, where parents and students read to each other regularly

ASSESSMENT (IN STUDENT PORTFOLIO)

~ Initial assessment of each child (again at the end of the first trimester):

- Letter recognition

- Beginning consonant sounds

- Sentence dictation ("I have a big dog at home.")

- Writing of upper- and lower-case letters

- List of twenty-five basic sight words

- Running record of reading leveled books

~ Eight single books on the basic colors, plus a review book: *I See Colors*

~ Individual page in class big book

~ Individual descriptive paragraphs

~ Individual book called *I Like Books*

~ Reading of poetry in notebook

~ Two number books (0–12, 13–20)

~ Journals

~ Running records of books in guided reading

RESOURCES

Big books from Macmillan Level 1, New York: Macmillan/McGraw Hill School Publishing

> *I Like Books,* Anthony Browne, 1988
>
> *Dawn by the Bay,* George Ancona, 1993
>
> *The Chick and the Duckling,* Mirra Ginsburg, 1972
>
> *My Friends,* Taro Gomi, 1989
>
> *Rain,* Robert Kalan, 1998
>
> *One More Monday,* Uri Shulevity, 1967
>
> *Together,* George Ella Lyon, 1989

Poems (nursery rhymes, counting, friends, fall, and so forth)

Technology (Living Books, Minnesota Educational Computer Consortium program on beginning sounds)

Guest readers (parents, grandparents, principal, community people, retired teachers)

Aliki. *How a Book Is Made.* New York: HarperCollins, 1986

Areglado, Nancy and Mary Dill. *Let's Write: A Practical Guide to Teaching Writing in the Early Grades.* New York: Scholastic, 1997

Bang, Molly. *Ten, Nine, Eight.* New York: Scholastic, 1983

Christelow, Eileen. *What Do Authors Do?* Boston: Houghton Mifflin, 1995

Boxes of books from Keystone Area Educational Agency

Books from the school library

Books from other teachers

Student books from home

Leveled books for guided reading

FIRST GRADE NEWSLETTER
SEPTEMBER
MRS. GILL

Our First Expedition

Our first expedition, Books! Books! Books! will begin Monday, September 15, with a kickoff by Dr. Hall reading his favorite children's book in costume. During this expedition your child will be immersed in the exciting world of books and will include a trip to the Carnegie Stout Library in October. Requests for drivers will be coming soon. Please remember that an insurance form is needed for all drivers.

Your child will be involved in making class books and many individual books during this expedition that he/she will read to you, themselves, and others. We are planning to "buddy up" with older students to read to them too.

This expedition stresses language arts, but it will also include science and social studies outcomes. In science your child will sort out many objects by various properties. Social studies will focus on friendship within the expedition.

Bring a Favorite Book to School!

Please help your child choose a favorite book from home to bring to school on Monday, September 15. Please write your child's name inside the book. We will use the book for several different activities and it may need to stay at school for several weeks.

Read at Home Daily

This expedition will also kick off a reading at home program. Reading aloud to your child is the best way to help at home. As little as ten minutes a day does wonders. Please read one book every day to your child and fill out the green sheet accompanying the book in the white DB&T bags. Your child should return the book every day for a new book. Any and all books that you read to your child or he/she reads can be recorded on the green sheet. This reading at home program will continue all school year. Thank you for helping your child to enjoy books.

First Grade News

Reading at Home

All children are encouraged to check out a new book daily from the classroom library to be read at home. Many thanks to all the parents for reading to your child. Research has proven that reading to your child is the BEST way to help your child succeed in school. Many children have already read 30–40 books. Continue looking for their white DB&T bags for books to read together. Books should be returned daily for a new one.

Reading at School

Together, we can help your child learn to read. Here at school, your child participates in one of five guided reading groups. A new book is chosen and read daily in class. The focus is enjoyment of the story, comprehension, phonics, learning basic sight words, and using reading cues.

During reading groups time the other children rotate through 6–7 learning centers such as computers, math, writing, art, ABC (phonics), listening, and reading.

Math

In math the children are learning how to write the numbers from 1–20 and trying to work on any reversed numbers. We are also learning the concept of adding and counting on 1, 2, and 3 with manipulatives and numerals. We are practicing counting by 2's. The children participate in calendar and weather discussions daily.

Expedition: Books, Books, Books

This expedition is progressing very well. So far, your child has made several books, including 8 on the colors, one called *I Like Books,* a class book about the trip to the library, and a class ABC book. To ensure their BEST work, we start with a practice copy of each page and they have learned how to critique each other's work. They make the piece better and then proceed to the final copy. Ask your child to say the chant called, Good, Better, Best.

I would also like to thank the parents who drove our class to the library: Mrs. Ann Hearn, Mrs. Annette Arnold, Mrs. Linda Ferguson, Mr. Mark Decker, and Mr. Steve Clemen.

I also thank those parents who volunteered to drive, but were not needed to drive this time. I will call on you to drive another time.

Science

Our class has started a science unit about the properties of objects. Students will be observing and classifying objects by color, shape, size, texture, and weight. They will also learn about objects that sink or float and experiment with magnifying glasses.

Parent-Teacher Conferences

I'm looking forward to seeing all of you on November 6th or 7th to discuss your child's progress and to show the portfolio of beautiful work. Please bring your first-grade child to the conference to participate in the celebration of good work.

Sincerely,
Mrs. Nora Gill

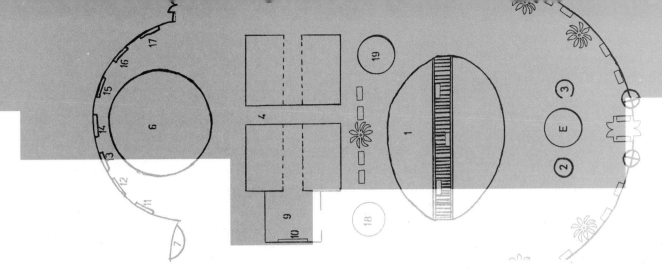

DREAM ON

KAREN MACDONALD AND PHIL DYER
King Middle School
Portland, Maine

*A*t the time the sixth-grade team began brainstorming ideas for our second expedition, "Dream On," our school had started preparing for a renovation that would add one new wing to the building and remodel the remaining classrooms. We already knew we wanted to develop a math-driven expedition. In previous expeditions it had been difficult to include math, and we did not want to force the subject in if it did not make sense. Giving the students the opportunity to have a direct impact on the architectural project allowed us to focus on the math and make the expedition realistic to the students. We also thought that students should have a say in the design of the building that would serve middle school students, so we centered "Dream On" on this premise.

That first year we charged the students with designing their vision for a sixth-grade wing in the renovated school. In teams, students created their own architectural firms, designating names and creating a letterhead for correspondence. The expedition required a great deal of direct instruction in math class. Students studied area and perimeter, as well as the relationship between the two. We covered geometry terms as well as the effective use of angles and shapes for interior design. Several miniprojects led the students through instruction on drawing to scale. The final instruction for the floor plan included a set maximum area (35,000 square feet) and a fixed scale of one inch to eight feet. Using their math skills of measurement and geometry, the teams drafted floor plans of proposed wings and wrote accompanying proposals.

The students gave their final presentation to the architects designing the building at the time. The real-world expectations set by the presence of the architects, and the possibility that any of the student teams could influence the building design, helped make the expedition a great success. When we heard the students' presentations in the library that year, it was one of those days when we were incredibly proud to be teaching.

Of course, in retrospect many things needed improvement the second time around. For instance, we did not include as much ongoing reflection as we would have liked. But the next year the biggest problem we faced when we considered doing this expedition with our next group of sixth graders was the fact that now the renovation was under way, and we could not tell the students that they would have a real impact on this project. The "real life" aspect of the expedition was gone.

We still wanted to adapt this expedition for a new group of students because we had found the topic of architecture so engaging for students and perfectly suited for interdisciplinary teaching. So, after a great deal of brainstorming, we came up with the idea of having students design their vision for a Gulf of Maine Aquarium. This proposed project had been in the local news for several years. Supporters of the aquarium were having a difficult time finding public interest, as well as financial support. We now could incorporate science into this expedition, since students would learn about aquatic animals and habitats. Finally, we had returned the "real life" aspect to our expedition.

Our team has completed the expedition twice with the focus on the aquarium design. Both efforts have been enormously successful in terms of the motivation and learning of the students. We started these expeditions at the beginning of November and completed both during the second week of January. Again, we believe that each time we work on an expedition we bring additional quality to our work. At the same time, we know that the students gain from seeing the models of students' work from past years, and that those examples help push them to improve the quality of their work.

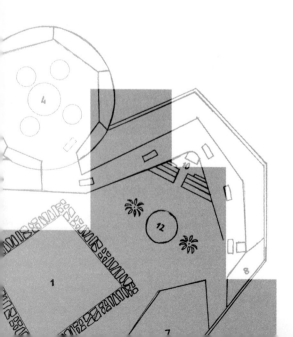

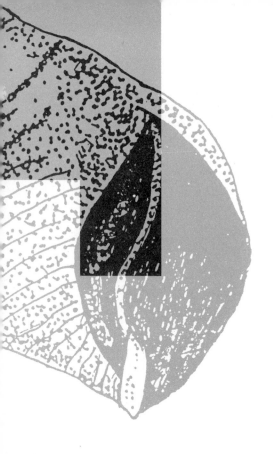

As we work through this expedition, all of the teachers in the house (Chris Griffin, Kim Verreault, Steve Morgenstein, and Mike Lynch, in addition to the two authors) play a role in its success. Although most of the content of the expedition is focused on science, math, language arts, and computer classes, everyone, including the social studies teacher, coaches students in their important project work. We have learned that to make a successful expedition you need to provide long periods of time for students to focus on their work. This requires everyone's cooperation and flexibility. When the students are drafting their floor plans, we all provide time in our classes for them to stay put and focus on their work. When the architects come in to critique their work, everyone turns their class over to this important activity. All six of the teachers share the time-consuming work of editing proposals with the students. Our students definitely benefit from the unity of the teachers. We are all focused on providing the support and instruction they need to complete this project successfully.

As we look to the future of this expedition, we realize that we may need to make a significant change in our focus. The Gulf of Maine Aquarium may soon become a reality for Portland, and the expedition will then lose its "real life" component. Currently, a bill is pending before the legislature that would provide funding for applied research at the new aquarium. In addition, private donations have provided the project with important support. However, many aspects of this expedition can be adapted to other authentic projects, and we look forward to the opportunities these future adventures will provide our students. "Dream On" has set the standard for us in terms of what a successful expedition can bring to the classroom.

The following Plan Outline provides more detail about "Dream On." The expedition was divided into phases that move from skill building to more advanced projects, culminating in the development of floor plans, and the final presentation. To define our learning goals, we use some terminology of the Portland Public Schools and King Middle School:

Learning Expectations
These are broad statements describing what students should know and be able to do when they graduate from the Portland Public Schools.

Content Standards
These are statements providing further definition of "Learning Expectations," describing the essential K–12 learning in the content area.

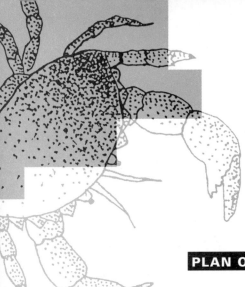

Key Learnings

These further describe the content standard. They also identify specific competencies.

Product Descriptor

This is a term used by the King faculty for the list of criteria or qualities required in a major project.

PLAN OUTLINE

TOPIC

During "Dream On" the students study aquatic animals and their habitats, as well as geometry and measurement as it relates to architecture. They then design an aquarium for Portland, Maine, based on this knowledge.

GUIDING QUESTIONS

~ How do the needs of aquatic animals impact the design of an aquarium?

~ What design elements of an aquarium would effectively engage middle school-age children?

~ How do architects combine specific measurement requirements and creativity to meet the needs of a client?

LEARNING GOALS

Learning Expectations

Each student will become:

~ a knowledgeable person

~ an effective communicator

~ a quality producer

- ∼ a versatile thinker
- ∼ a self-directed learner
- ∼ an involved citizen

Content Standards

Each student:

- ∼ uses reading skills and strategies to comprehend, interpret, and evaluate what is read
- ∼ uses the skills and strategies of the writing process for reflective, creative, and informational purposes
- ∼ demonstrates competence in speaking and listening tools for learning
- ∼ locates, retrieves, and records information from a variety of print and electronic sources
- ∼ interprets and evaluates information
- ∼ presents and communicates information for a variety of audiences
- ∼ understands and applies methods of measurement
- ∼ understands and applies the concept of geometry and spatial sense
- ∼ understands the operations, tools, and uses of technology
- ∼ understands the life cycle, behavior, and structure of various organisms

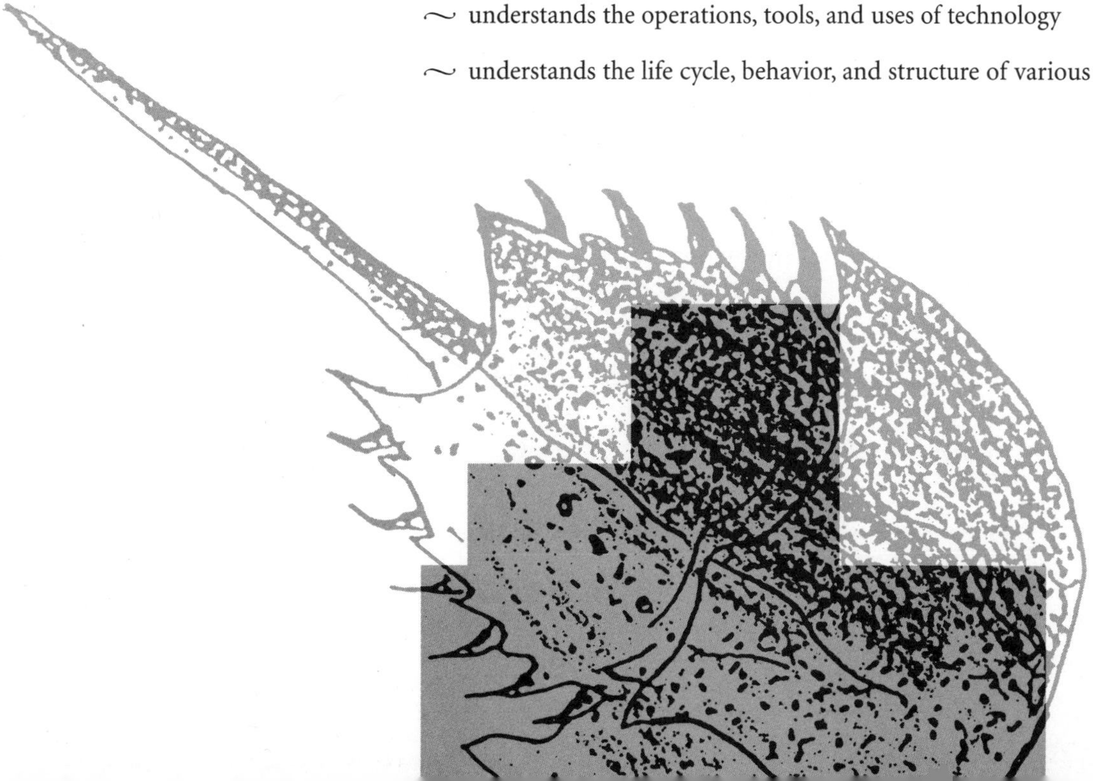

Complex Thinking Standards

Each student will practice these skills:

~ Induction

~ Constructing support

~ Decision making

~ Invention

~ Comparison

Phase One

Project

Developing proposal and presentation of sites for Gulf of Maine Aquarium

Activity 1

Students traveled to the five proposed Portland sites for the Gulf of Maine Aquarium.

Key Learning

1. Applies information from graphs, charts, tables, and photos

Activity 2

Students drafted a short written narrative about each site, including their response to the criteria. The narrative contained the advantages and disadvantages of each proposed site.

Key Learnings

1. Writes for public and private audiences

2. Provides evidence for a claim

3. Understands and uses elements of good writing

Activity 3

Students presented their site to the rest of the students. Presentations included pros and cons of the sites.

Key Learnings

1. Makes formal presentations to the class

2. Uses presentation techniques

Activity 4
Students voted on the site they thought would be the most effective after hearing each presentation.

Key Learnings

1. Identifies important criteria for assessing alternatives

2. Identifies the extent to which each alternative possesses each criterion

3. Makes a selection that meets the decision criteria and answers the initial decision question

Phase Two

Project
Conducting a survey of the New England Aquarium

Activity 1
Students reviewed the survey sheet that they would complete. The purpose of each question was discussed, and students had the opportunity to discuss any other aspect of the aquarium they wanted to focus on.

Key Learning

1. Reads for a variety of purposes

Activity 2
Students were presented with information on the Behind the Scenes Tour at the New England Aquarium. They were invited to submit an application, as only a small group of students could attend.

Key Learnings

1. Writes for public and private audiences

2. Writes in a variety of genres

Activity 3

Students visited the New England Aquarium, completing the survey sheet, which focused on their reaction to the architectural aspects and the educational aspects of the exhibits.

Key Learnings

1. Understands the need to access information relevant to a specific assignment

2. Selects items to compare

3. Selects characteristics on which to base the comparison

4. Identifies the similarities and differences among the items, using the identified characteristics

Phase Three: Getting Started in Math

Activities

As "Dream On" began, math class focused on the skills needed for architectural drafting. During the first few weeks of the expedition, students learned about area, perimeter, geometry, drawing to scale, how to use architectural tools, and the function of line weights and universal symbols. The expectation was that students would include applications of the mathematical concepts in their proposal.

Key Learnings

1. Demonstrates a working knowledge of appropriate geometric vocabulary

2. Recognizes and uses angle relationships

3. Understands and defines length, width, height, weight, perimeter, area, volume, time, and temperature

4. Selects measurement units and tools required in a particular situation

Phase Four: Getting Started in Language Arts

Project

Creating a company and designing logo, business cards, and business letter

Activity 1

Students were asked to imagine that they were the president of their own architectural company. They created a company name and logo and designed business cards on the computer.

Key Learnings

1. Refines and develops keyboarding skills

2. Uses technology to accomplish tasks

Activity 2

Students composed business letters to Don Perkins, president of the Gulf of Maine Aquarium Committee, persuading him to take a close look at their aquarium design and proposal.

Key Learnings

1. Understands and uses elements of the writing process

2. Writes for public and private audiences

3. Uses planning, drafting, and revision to produce a finished piece of work

4. Uses a variety of sentence structures

Phase Five: Getting Started in Science

Project

Research aquatic habitats

Activity 1

During the first stages of the expedition in science, the students researched aquatic habitats in preparation for designing their own aquariums. Research time on the Internet also allowed everyone to visit fantastic aquarium sites around the world.

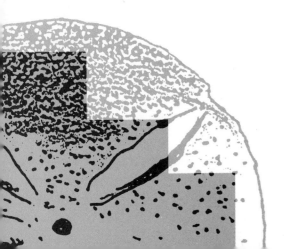

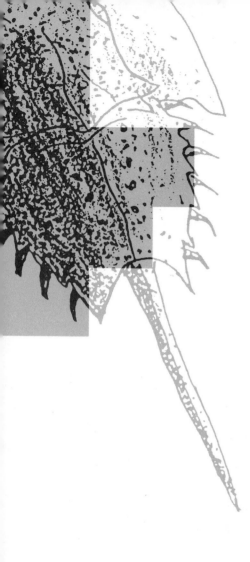

Key Learnings

1. Understands the need to access information relevant to a specific assignment

2. Recognizes the need to adjust strategies, locate additional information, or re-examine information when necessary

Activity 2
Students completed facts sheets on five aquatic habitats that they researched.

Key Learning

1. Understands the life cycle, behavior, and structure of various organisms

Activity 3
Students used their research information to complete five exhibit outlines. The exhibit design needed to be based on the habits and habitat of the animals in the tank or exhibition area.

Key Learning

1. Understands the life cycle, behavior, and structure of various organisms

Phase Six
Presentation by Joe Hemmes, a local architect, on his proposal for a Fort Gorges Aquarium. He modeled the type of presentation the students would give later in the expedition.

Phase Seven

Project
Writing a proposal

Activities
Students spent several weeks writing the proposal that would accompany their floor plans. Rough draft proposals were typed, rewritten, and retyped, and on and on ....

Key Learnings

1. Understands and uses the elements of the writing process

2. Writes for public and private audiences

3. Uses planning, drafting, and revision to produce a finished piece of work

4. Uses a variety of sentence structures

5. Understands and uses elements of good writing

Phase Eight

Project
Developing rough drafts of floor plans

Activities
Student work on their floor plans coincided with work on the proposals. It was during this time that students had to put their new knowledge of scale, area, perimeter, and volume to the test. Everyone was responsible for making sure that the exhibits in their aquarium were designed with precision.

Key Learning

1. Selects measurement units and tools required in a particular situation

Phase Nine

Professional Critique

Activity
Professional architects from the area looked at each floor plan with a critical eye. Their role was to give feedback to the students before the final revisions were made.

Key Learnings

1. Uses planning, drafting, and revision to produce a finished piece of work

2. Demonstrates the habits of continuous improvement

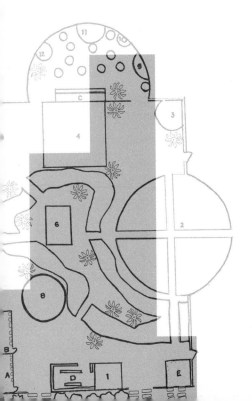

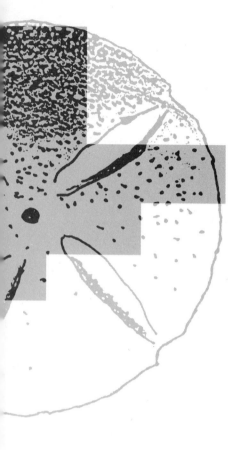

Phase Ten

Project

Producing final drafts of proposals and floor plans

Activity 1

Students completed the final drafts of their floor plans and proposals.

Key Learnings

1. Understands standard bibliographic format

2. Uses planning, drafting, and revision to produce a finished piece of work

3. Creates products that are purposeful and meaningful to an audience

4. Creates products that exhibit quality

Activity 2

Students used the product descriptors for the floor plans and the proposals to self-evaluate their work.

Key Learning

1. Demonstrates the ability to self-assess

Phase Eleven

Classroom Presentation

Activity 1

Students from each of the four classrooms participating in the expedition presented their floor plans and proposals to classmates through an oral presentation.

Key Learnings

1. Makes formal presentations to the class

2. Uses presentation techniques

Activity 2

After listening to all the presenters in their class, each group voted for the four students they believed would best represent them in front of a larger audience.

Key Learning

1. Makes a selection that meets the decision criteria

Phase Twelve

"Final 16" Present to a Large Community Audience

Activity

Sixteen students presented their work to an audience of fellow students, parents, community members, teachers, and administrators, as well as to Don Perkins, president of the Gulf of Maine Aquarium Committee.

Key Learning

1. Creatively and purposefully presents information in a style and tone that effectively capitalize on the level of knowledge, understanding, and interest of the audience

Phase Thirteen

Assessment Conferencing

Activity

Each student met individually with two teachers to review and discuss his or her work during this expedition. Reflection sheets were completed by the students prior to the conference.

Key Learning

1. Demonstrates the ability to self-assess

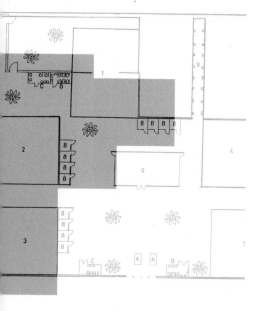

Phase Fourteen

Gulf of Maine Aquarium Committee Connects with Windsor-6 Students

Activity

Sixteen students participated in an open forum with the committee of twenty community members. The committee actually incorporated some of the students' designs into their guidelines for the architects. The architects came back to the group of sixteen for a critiquing session. The students gave feedback to the architects on their first draft of the actual plans for the aquarium. (Quite a turnabout!) Finally, two students have joined the Gulf of Maine Aquarium Committee and attend monthly meetings. These students provide monthly updates to all of us. The committee is in the process of securing funding for the project.

Key Learnings

1. Communicates with a variety of audiences

2. Communicates for a variety of purposes

Ongoing Assessment

There were multiple opportunities for ongoing assessment and reflection during this expedition:

1. Teacher editing conferences held with students during Phase Seven

2. Teacher conferences with students regarding their floor plan held during Phase Eight

3. Critiques from professional architects held during Phase Nine

4. Completion of product descriptor ratings by students during Phase Eleven

FINAL ASSESSMENTS

1. Individual conferences with each student

2. Final pieces that were graded (based on product descriptors)

- floor plan

- business letter

- proposal

- oral presentation

- expedition portfolio of research and rough drafts

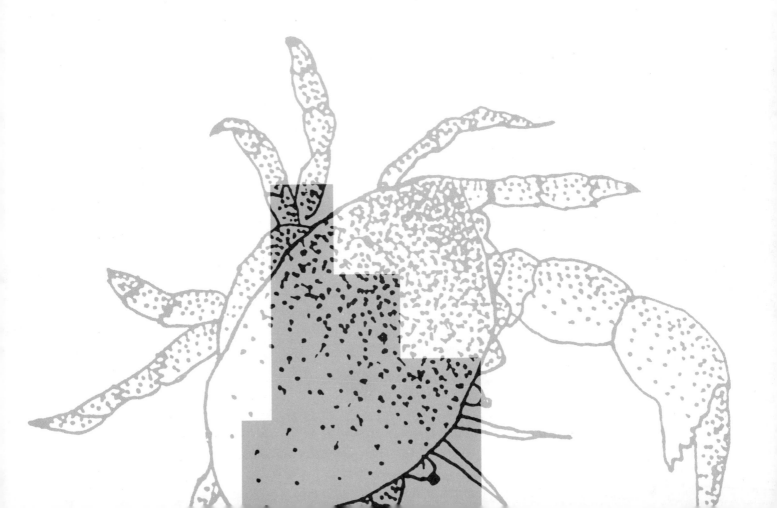

RESOURCES

Books and Magazines

Chinery, Michael, et al., eds. *Illustrated Encyclopedia of Animals.* New York: Kingfisher Books, 1992.

Hannau, Hans. *In the Coral Reef.* New York: Doubleday, 1974.

Leon, Vicki, ed. *The Kelp Forest.* San Luis Obispo, Calif.: Blake Publishing, 1990.

Levine, Joseph. *Undersea Life.* New York: Steward, Tabori & Chang, 1985.

Monterey Bay Aquarium. Monterey, Calif.: Monterey Bay Aquarium Foundation, 1992.

Taylor, Dave. *Endangered Ocean Animals.* New York: Crabtree Publishing, 1993.

Taylor, Dave. *Endangered Wetland Animals.* New York: Crabtree Publishing, 1992.

Taylor, Leighton. *Aquariums—Windows to Nature.* Englewood Cliffs, N.J.: Prentice Hall, 1993.

Tayntor, Elizabeth. *Dive to the Coral Reef.* New York: Crown, 1986.

Wilson, Barbara. *Icebergs and Glaciers.* San Luis Obispo, Calif.: Blake Publishing, 1990.

Wood, Jenny. *Coral Reefs.* New York: Scholastic, 1991.

World of Water. Boston: New England Aquarium, 1990.

Wright, Alexandra. *At Home in the Tide Pool.* Watertown, Mass.: Charlesbridge Publishing, 1992.

Zoobooks Magazine. Wildlife Education Ltd. (Issues on Sea Otters, Seabirds, Turtles, Dolphins, Porpoises, Sharks, Whales, Penguins)

Experts and Fieldwork

Local architects

Possible construction sites for the Gulf of Maine Aquarium

New England Aquarium

Huntley Architect Design Corporation
1234 Penny Lane
San Jose, California 96123

December 12, 1996

Gulf of Marine Aquarium Committee
Attn: Mr. Don Perkins
P.O. Box 7549
Portland, Maine 04112

Dear Mr. Perkins:

Are you looking for an experienced aquarium designer? If so, you have found your company. H.A.D. Corp. has designed many important buildings such as: the Empire State Building, the C.N. Tower, and many others. Our company is an award winning architectural firm. In 1973, we won the Universal Architect Award.

We won the School of Modern Architects Award in 1994, and we received the United States Architects of the Millennium Award in 1919.

Experience is what we are all about. Our firm was founded in 1901. Since then, we have always been on time and affordable. We have thirty-eight engineers, twelve marine biologists, and forty-five architects. Nine of our architects specialize in aquariums. H.A.D. Corp. has built many aquariums similar to what Maine is looking for.

Please take the time to read our proposal. Here at H.A.D. Corp., we know you will be greatly impressed.

Sincerely,

a. Huntley

Aaron Huntley,
President, Huntley Architect Design Corporation

SUNRISE
Architectural Designers

13 Los Rios Drive
Santa Fe, New Mexico 53298
Tel: (505)237-0600 Fax: (505)237-0500

December 10, 1996

Gulf of Maine Aquarium Committee
Attn: Mr. Don Perkins
P.O. Box 7549
Portland, Maine 04112

Dear Mr. Perkins:

Are you looking for experience? Our firm has designed over four hundred buildings and we have had more than four hundred extremely satisfied customers. Sunrise Architectural Designers have designed nine aquariums and three out of the nine aquariums were in cold climates. Our corporation was started in 1978, and as you can see, we have had lots of experience in designing.

Sunrise Architectural Designers have won many awards including the Golden Spaces Award and National Designers Award for three years straight. We combine uniqueness with functionality and appeal to create our own original designs. Our work is always within budget and completed before the deadline.

Research is important to our firm. We have talked to many students and teachers and they have given us lots of good ideas that we have incorporated in our design for the Gulf of Maine Aquarium. Our design will appeal to all age groups.

Thank you for reading our proposal. If you have any questions at all about anything please feel free to call us. I believe that Sunrise Architectural Designers can do a fabulous job with this project and leave you feeling more than satisfied.

Sincerely,

Lindsay Rowe

Lindsay Rowe
President, Sunrise Architectural Designers

The Gulf of Maine Aquarium

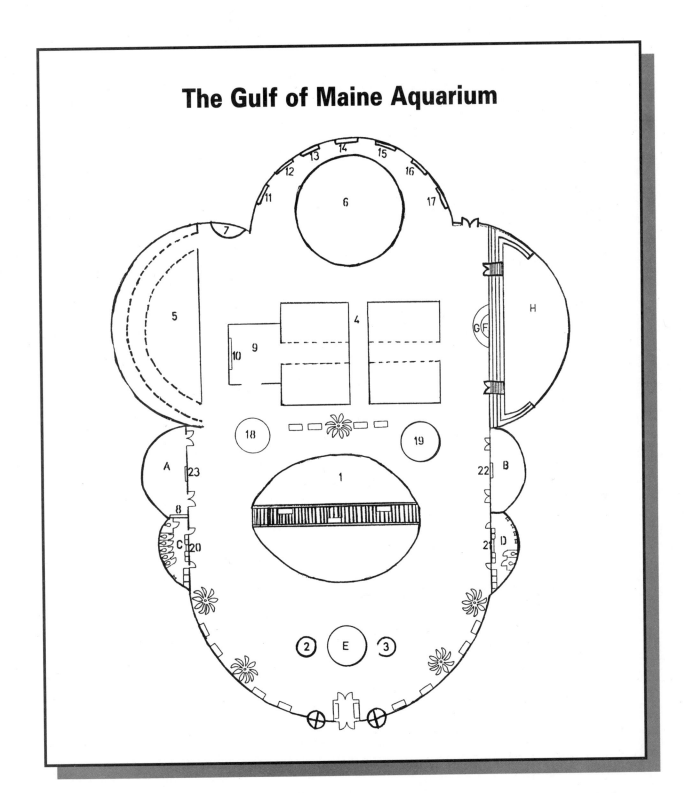

INVESTIGATIONS

ANGELA BUDDE AND SARAH JOHNSON
Fulton Intermediate School
Dubuque, Iowa

*A*s visitors crossed our classroom, they entered a world filled with the sound of birds, a rustic barn, an icy mountain, and a cypress swamp. Their eyes widened, their jaws dropped, and students jumped to attention. As they scanned the room, they saw papier-mâché birds constructed and painted to look like birds we would see in nature. There were leaves, vines, trees, and rivers everywhere the eye could see. The fifth-grade students had transformed this once ordinary classroom, at Fulton Intermediate School in Dubuque, Iowa, top to bottom into a bird sanctuary limited only by their imaginations. The students were eager to share their work. On cue, our visitors began meandering along the "yellow brick road" running through the sanctuary. This led to individual habitats where students stood at attention behind lecterns holding the bird books they had written. Students enthusiastically shared the information in their bird books, fielded questions, and beamed with pride.

The "Investigations" expedition was born out of a need to teach our district's science curriculum in a meaningful, inquiry-based way. We began looking at what we knew the students needed to be able to do, what our personal areas of interest were, and what resources were available to us. The fifth-grade science curriculum required us to teach about birds. In an effort to incorporate as much of the fifth-grade science curriculum as possible, we pulled concepts from the existing microscopes and pond life unit. We realized that our fifth graders needed to know, for example, how to use a simple microscope and identify the different parts of a cell. It seemed a natural fit that we could teach these as we explored the topic of birds and their environment.

Through the investigations of birds, we wanted the students to explore the scientific process—the process of trial, error, learning from the data they gather, and trying again. In our adult lives and work places, these are skills that we rely on. Students were to formulate hypotheses about bird characteristics such as foot types, beaks, eyes, feathers, and bones. Using their hypotheses, students developed and conducted experiments that allowed them to collect data, test their predictions, and then summarize and record their observations on lab report forms.

One example of such a project occurred as students realized that there were different types of feathers on a bird. We gave them feathers, and then we brainstormed as a class why birds might need different types of feathers. In small groups, they used a teacher-provided lab form and designed simple experiments to prove hypotheses. As we walked around observing the groups, we viewed feathers being dropped from high places simultaneously to see which feather would catch the wind. Some students even taped groups of feathers together, flapped them wildly, and felt for differences in air movement, all the while vigorously recording their data in their notebooks. Although most experiments contained flaws, this provided a great opportunity to discuss variables and invalid conclusions. Finally, it was decided that down feathers were for warmth, contour feathers for flight.

While lab reports offered students the opportunity to record information in an organized fashion, we thought that writing needed to be a stronger component of this expedition. Our students needed to be immersed in the writing process, and through the authoring of expository bird books they received this opportunity. This gave us a chance to have students collect information on a bird of their choice from various resources to organize their information on tower strategies (a writing tool that allows students to graphically organize and outline ideas), and then compile and publish an expository book. We required students to create multiple written and illustrative drafts, peer revise, edit, and critique the multiple drafts until they accomplished their own personal best.

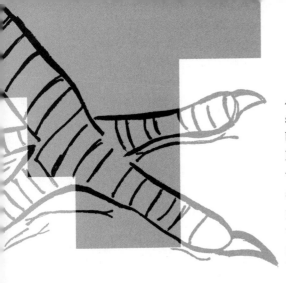

As we completed the different topics such as anatomy and environment, the students excavated mountains of useful information on birds to write their books. They diligently surfed the Internet, browsed resources in our school library, and picked through Area Education Association boxed books. It was imperative that students know how to get the most out of what was available to them. We discussed tables of contents, indexes, glossaries, and picture captions. Students' reading was not limited to researching. Along with reading information on birds, students also joined in reading the class novel, *My Side of the Mountain*, written by Jean Craighead George. This book invited lively discussions on birds, captivity, and our environment. Before long students started to bring in news articles on birds, and we discussed current events surrounding birds. Students became motivated to read simply because they were hungry for more knowledge. All of this reading became useful not only as a vehicle for gathering information, but in also offering quality writing for students to review.

Armed with all this information, students began the grueling process of authoring the best paragraph possible for them. As we completed each topic on the birds, students repeated the process of researching, completing tower sheets, and writing as many as four drafts to attain their personal best. Every time students finished a paragraph, it got tucked safely into a folder where the book was slowly but surely coming together. There was serious celebration, by teachers and students, the day the final pages hit their folders and headed to the binding machine (especially from those few students who had felt all along that one draft said it all).

Throughout this process we pulled paragraph examples from student-authored books and read them out loud. Students began to talk the language of writing. They identified likes and dislikes (similes and metaphors), beautiful language (better known by most teachers as adjectives), and powerful verbs. They discovered, through their own experience as readers, what makes a reader want to read. We knew we wanted to include these in our books. From these discussions the class generated a peer-critique form for student critique sessions. We made revision and editing two separate steps, going so far as to do them on separate days with separate checklists, so the students were changing more than punctuation and spelling.

As birds became a large part of our fifth graders' lives during these months, we felt a natural flow taking us into the topic of the environment and our

influences on the environment. The students hatched and cared for live chickens in the classroom. This provided the opportunity to study the development of a growing embryo into a chick. When the eggs arrived, we shared Dr. Seuss's *Horton Hatches the Egg* and discussed our responsibility for the chicks. The students became invested in these chickens. We kept the eggs in the room, and the students had to monitor the temperature and moisture of the incubator as the eggs developed. As students prepared to leave one day, an excited yell rang out, "I hear peeping!" A flood of students rushed to the incubator. Sure enough, the eggs were wiggling and chicks were preparing to hatch. In an effort not to miss the blessed event altogether, we set up a video camera to record throughout the night. Fortunately, when students arrived the next morning, only one chick had hatched. Needless to say, the students and teachers spent the rest of that day peering into the incubator.

We felt that this was a teachable moment, and we began to discuss how humans can change the lives of real animals such as our chicks. One example was how pollutants could affect the eggshell. Our students also could easily relate to bald eagles, which are prevalent in our area. Students recognized the bald eagle as an endangered species, and the connection of pollutants causing this was easy to make. The students became more knowledgeable and sensitive to the world around them and to how people influence nature and its cycles. The students could perform little actions, such as not littering, to make the community a safer place for the birds who live here.

As they became aware, we began to discuss proactive things we could do for the birds in our area. The students' awareness allowed them to provide a better life for the birds in our community—this meant that the students designed and built bird feeders and houses that hung in our community. We encouraged the students to use recyclable materials from home and then work directly with a family member, giving the students an opportunity to share their knowledge. In retrospect, we believe we need to emphasize in the future that a hanging bird feeder is a lifelong commitment since the birds rely on that food. If our students do not feel they can commit to this, they need to find a community member who will take on that responsibility for them, whether that be a grandparent, a neighbor, or one of Fulton's business partners.

As we look back over this expedition, we see that some of the most successful components were the pieces that the students still talk about: staying late after hours to complete the sanctuary, publishing high-quality books by doing as many as four drafts per page, coming in during off-school hours to take care of the chicks, and playing Deadly Links, a Project Wild initiative in which students simulate the entrance of pesticides into the food chain and discover possible consequences of this action. We, as the teachers, are well aware that our students had an opportunity to work very hard and consequently see their own excellence and realize what they were truly capable of. Our hope is that they will take this knowledge and apply it to other learning opportunities in the future.

We saw the opportunity to teach students how to be learners instead of just teaching to the curriculum, by helping them build their repertoire of skills. We wanted our students to learn skills that would help them tackle any academic undertaking ahead of them. For example, we taught them how to write detailed plans when working on long-range projects. In order for a goal to be reached, a realistic plan must be developed and followed. These plans included sketches, narrative descriptions, a materials list, a very detailed "to do" list, and deadlines. The students also needed to work as team members, and communicate and work with others, which are skills used in the workplace, at home, and in their neighborhoods.

The first time we taught this expedition it was driven by our district standards. After we taught it, the students' passions and questions helped to drive the changes that seemed natural. There was a need for the students to feel more responsibility toward the environment and see birds as living creatures that depend on our choices for their survival. Along with this came a need to provide more quality writing experiences for all of our students, many of whom are considered to be at risk for dropping out of school. In our school, this constitutes approximately 75 percent of the students. The gathering of expedition models from previous years will help build quality in subsequent years. This expedition was so involving for our students that they became intrinsically motivated.

The younger students who had crossed the threshold as guests to this year's bird sanctuary will come to us next year with an enthusiasm to learn and be

part of the bird expedition. The question left ringing in our ears as our younger guests leave the sanctuary is "Do we get to do the bird thing?" With a smile, we always answer as enthusiastically as they ask. We know that each year brings new changes, new ideas, and a new bird expedition ready to unfold as the students weave threads of their own passions into the fabric of our existing expedition, making it as thrilling and exciting for us as it will be for them.

PLAN OUTLINE

TOPIC

Investigating the scientific method and birds

GUIDING QUESTIONS

~ How does the scientific process help us learn about our environment?

~ How do our actions affect other species?

~ What are the various characteristics of birds that make each species unique?

LEARNING GOALS

Students will understand:

~ the anatomy of a bird by creating accurate papier-mâché bird models and passing quizzes.

~ the various adaptations of bird anatomy, based on the habitat they live in, by designing and participating in experiments on beaks, feathers, feet, and bones.

~ the various components of individual habitats, by creating accurate habitats of the bird they studied in detail, creating the bird sanctuary as a culminating activity. These habitats would include vegetation, water source, nests, other animal life, enemies, and food sources.

the scientific process, in order to test hypotheses by designing experiments and following a lab format. Their conversations and reflective journal writing taking place following the activities needs to indicate that students understand variables and draw valid conclusions.

Students will practice and be able to:

~ make detailed and accurate sketches of their learning throughout the expedition—for example, the mammal bone versus bird bone, down versus contour feathers, a magnified view of feather parts, a cross-sectional view of a fertilized egg

~ take a large assignment and break it into smaller parts by writing and following a detailed plan

~ organize information by using a writing outline and organizer such as a tower strategy, and compiling the information into a book format

~ present material effectively to an audience of various ages

~ use library skills and multiple technology sources to locate information

Students will practice and develop qualities of character and community, including:

~ working as a team member (positively involving even reluctant team members, problem solving without adult intervention)

~ working independently without constant adult supervision

~ engaging in self-reflection

PROJECTS

Project One

The students created anatomically accurate clay or papier-mâché birds to display later in a class bird sanctuary.

Learning Goals

Students would consider proportion, attention to authentic detail, and realism in creating their birds and developing sketches in their bird lab books.

Major Activities/Tasks

Students researched beak type, foot type, feather color, and eye type to go into their bird books.

Specific Goals for Activities

Students created a bird of their choice to place in the habitat they would be constructing with the art teacher.

Ongoing Assessment

Students were assessed in art class as an opportunity to integrate specialists into the expedition.

Project Two

Students wrote individual or group expository bird books, which we critiqued and revised until they were of publishable quality.

Learning Goals

Students integrate technology into research and effectively use tower strategies to organize information. Students take this research and turn the information into paragraphs and finally a book that has a natural flow. Metaphors, similes, and descriptive writing have been taught in the past and were revisited in order to make the writing in their bird books come alive. This allowed us to build the language of writing and have wonderful discussions on literature. The students revised, critiqued, and edited drafts of their illustrations for the bird book, emphasizing proportion, perspective, and attention to detail. As an enrichment opportunity, some students wrote glossaries as well.

Ongoing Assessment

Prior to writing, students created a rubric based on models they critiqued which was used throughout the writing process.

Project Three

Students in teams constructed a detailed bird sanctuary in the classroom based on their research.

Learning Goals

Students wrote plans that included a materials list, a daily "to do" list, sketches, written descriptions, and deadlines. Students worked as effective and productive team members. Finally, students used a variety of artistic resources to create a habitat that took into consideration scale and proportion and was supposed to simulate an actual habitat.

Major Activities/Tasks

Students researched habitats for types of vegetation, water sources, other animals, and enemies. They wrote and revised their plans of action and followed daily "to do" lists to complete their habitat by their deadline. Students also set up a route through the various habitats and built cardboard stands to hold their bird books through their presentation.

Specific Goals for Activities and Tasks

Students created a realistic habitat that would house their bird and give them a format for sharing their writing and showing their understanding of habitat. Students built teamwork skills.

Ongoing Assessment

Students were assessed throughout the writing of their plan regarding the accuracy and authenticity of the habitat that they were going to create. Students completed a teamwork rubric on an almost daily basis to reflect on their self-participation and sometimes on the participation of another team member. They were accountable each day to an adult and to teammates for the work specified in the plan.

ASSESSMENT

Culminating Performance

~ The habitat was open to the public, which included the rest of our school, parents, extended family, and staff.

~ Students orally presented their bird books to visitors. They stood at attention in their habitats behind their cardboard bookstands and fielded questions regarding their habitat and chosen bird.

Assessing Students' Overall Achievement

We created student-generated rubrics prior to the writing of our books and the construction of our sanctuary. This determined what our class felt was quality work. Within a class discussion we talked about what it would take to be the best team member we could be, and we shared with them a team rubric that we then decided to use as the basis of our self-reflection. The use of portfolios allowed us to assess authentically the student's work, balancing grading with comments on a selection of student work and reflections.

RESOURCES

Books

Atwood, Margaret. *For the Birds.* Toronto: Douglas & McIntyre, 1990.

Cohen, Sharon A. *Bird Nests.* San Francisco: Collins Publishers, 1993.

Cole, Joanna. *A Chick Hatches.* New York: Morrow, 1976.

Jeunesse, Gallimard, and Pascale de Bourgoing. *The Egg: A First Discovery Book.* New York: Scholastic, 1992.

Jeunesse, Gallimard, Claude Delafosse, and Rene Mettler. *Birds: A First Discovery Book.* New York: Scholastic, 1993.

Petty, Kate. *Birds of Prey.* New York: Shooting Star Press, 1995.

Roberts, M.L. *World's Weirdest Birds.* Mahwah, N.J.: Troll Associates, 1996.

We also used Area Education Association resources and our public library to obtain multiple bird books for student research.

Films

The students had the opportunity to view a number of films on the topic, including:

Through the Seasons with Birds: Fall and *Through the Seasons with Birds: Winter,* filmed and produced by Maslowski Wildlife Productions, Evanston, Ill.: Altschul Group, 1994.

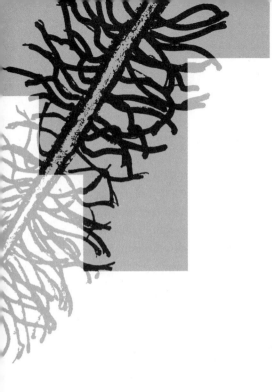

Experts

Army Corps of Engineers

Department of Natural Resources

Local college biology professor

Local owners of an emu farm

A teacher's spouse, Tom Syke, who raises chickens

Fieldwork Sites

Eagle Watch at the Lock and Dam: This gave students an opportunity to help the Department of Natural Resources by counting eagles

Swiss Valley Nature Center and Park

E. B. Lyons Nature Center

"Eco Meet," sponsored by the Department of Natural Resources, where four students received a daylong enrichment opportunity to study eagles, forestry, the Mississippi River, and water safety

Loras College

REFLECTIONS

Timeline

This expedition lasted four months. We devoted about two hours per day to it, but this was flexible. As we saw the need to spend more time, we would work on the expedition for the greater part of the day. We spent approximately two months' worth of time in the teaching of content and another two months on the completion of the culminating bird book and sanctuary projects. We taught a concept using various activities for approximately two days, and then the students authored a paragraph on this concept of their bird. Students spent approximately five days in the process of writing and illustrating each page. The last two weeks of our expedition were spent planning and building the sanctuary. The service component was completed with families outside of school time.

Immersion

The greatest immersion activity for this expedition is having the students from the lower grades come through our sanctuary. They come to us in the fall asking, "Do we get to do that sanctuary thing like you did last year?" In short, they are ready and willing from the start. We begin the expedition with a brainstorm session using a web, KWL charts (what do you Know? what do you Want to know? what have you Learned?), and a motivational reading entitled "Do You Have the Sense of a Goose?" Along with this comes the opportunity to scan books and choose a bird of interest in art class.

Parent Involvement

During our community circle time, our students author a weekly letter to parents updating them on the goings-on in our room. This is our opportunity to request help and resources and to encourage parent participation. This also gives the parents a tool for conversing with their child and to become familiar with the language of our classroom.

Design Principles

The Expeditionary Learning Outward Bound design principles have been carefully taken into consideration in our planning and teaching. We have chosen pieces from our expedition that are examples of these principles and compiled them into Showcase Portfolios, which children carry with them from grade to grade. Students have rewritten the design principles in their own words and displayed them in our room, referring to them often.

Enclosed you will find a showcase portfolio. This has been assembled by the fifth grade students in Mrs. Johnson's room from their hanging portfolios which we have used to collect samples of their work in all year long. We have taken the time to revisit the 10 design principles of Expeditionary Learning and what they mean to each of us in our daily lives here at Fulton School. Then, we have chosen pieces of work collected throughout the year which shows our best example of that design principle. Everyone has chosen different pieces and reflected as to what they have learned from them and how they fit within the design principle.

This is showcasing what each student feels is their best work. I would like all parents to look at them and discuss them with your child. Then I would like you to sign this letter to let me know you have had this opportunity. The students are required to return their portfolios to school before the end of this school year. I will house all of the portfolios in my classroom over the summer. In the Fall we will revisit them and set goals for ourselves for the new school year. By the end of 6th grade we will add at least 10 more pieces of our best work that we've saved over our 6th grade year. I am hopeful this will show great growth and learning and will give the students another opportunity to reflect on the type of learner they are, their strengths and weaknesses, and their interests.

Armed with this knowledge they will be required to present the entire portfolio to a panel of junior high teachers before the end of the 6th grade school year. They will not only be showing them their work and the growth they've made over the last two years but will also be expected to discuss what they have learned about themselves and how they are prepared to go onto junior high.

We feel this is an excellent opportunity for students to learn, grow, reflect on their accomplishments and set goals for themselves. ENJOY!

Sarah Johnson

Julie Gottschall
PARENT SIGNATURE

Peer Revision Conference

STUDENT 1: _____

STUDENT 2: _____

STOP!! REMEMBER!! Everyone is trying their hardest and doing their best. Comment in an appropriate tone of voice and be kind. It takes courage to share our writing. Along with this, remember we don't write for ourselves. We write for a designated audience. What we find interesting our audience may not. So listen to your audience when they suggest changes.

1. Give a specific positive comment about their paragraph.

2. Does the paragraph make sense? Or were there certain sentences that need rewording? If so, list the sentence numbers that need to be worked on. Give them some ideas.

3. Put a star where you become bored. Give two things they could add to help make it more interesting.

     1.

     2.

4. Circle all describing words. If less than two, help them add so they can have at least four.

5. Do they have it in a logical order? Is it in the order stated on the tower sheet? If not, what do they need to move?

6. What question(s) do you have after reading this paragraph? You MUST write down one question you would like answered.

7. Sentence starters. If they have more than two that are the same you need to help them to change the starters. (Write down each sentence beginning here.)

Now take all these suggestions and revise your paragraph to make it more pleasing to your AUDIENCE.

Reflection Questions

1. What was the most powerful learning experience you had in this expedition? Why was it so powerful?

2. If you were to do this whole expedition over, what would you, as a student, do differently? Example: Would you take more time on your lab book? Would you contribute more to your group? WHY would you do this differently?

3. How do you think this expedition will help you in the future? (for example, research skills, group skills, bird knowledge, microscopes)

4. During which activity do you feel your group best accomplished your goals. Why?

5. Think back to the group goal you wrote on your name posters. If you had to rate your group from one to ten on whether or not you made progress, what rating would you give yourself? Why? Provide specific examples that support this.

6. What one skill did you learn during this expedition that will be helpful to you in the future? Make sure it is not something you already knew. How will it be helpful? (Example: researching from several sources, drawing with detail, writing scientific experiment procedures.)

7. What was most challenging about this expedition? Why?

8. If you had the opportunity to do this expedition all over again, would you? Why or why not?

9. If you came back to 5-J next year to give the class advice on this expedition, what would you tell them and why?

10. What one social skill do you feel we as a class really need to focus on from now to the end of the year? Why? Come up with one as a class.

Ashley   4-4-97

                    First Draft

A Hoopoe's foot (assists) when he or she looks for its food. The type of Hoopoe's feet is called a scratcher. ~~They use their feet when they are on the ground and then they scratch at the ground and the food comes up.~~ When a Hoopoe scratches at the ground they use their feet to (dig) and pick things out. A scratchers foot looks like two toes in front and two toes in back. The color of Hoopoe's feet are brownish orange. Some other birds with the same feet are Peacocks, Pheasnts and Japennse Cranes. Birds (depend) on their feet when they (search) for food. Either to (scratch) at the ground or pick up their prey like Osprey do.

A Hoopoe's foot assists when he or she looks for its food. The type of a Hoopoe's foot is called a scratcher. When a Hoopoe scratches at the ground they use their feet to dig and pick things out. A scratcher foot has three toes in front and a small toe in the back. Scratcher feet are sort of used like a rake. Hoopoe's use their feet when they get their food off the ground. They scratch at the ground and food comes up for them. Brownish orange is the color of the Hoopoe's feet. Some other birds with the same feet are Peacocks, Pheasants, and Japanese Cranes. Most birds depend on their feet when they search for food, either to scratch at the ground or pick up their prey like Osprey do.

BIRD LIST

1. Snowy Owl
2. Great Horned Owl
3. Emperor Penguin
4. Adelle Penguin
5. Emu
6. Ostrich
7. Peregrine Falcon
8. Peacock
9. Flamingo
10. Canadian Goose
11. Snow Goose
12. Trumpeter Swan
13. Scarlet Ibis
14. Bald Eagle
15. Great Blue Heron
16. Brown Pelican
17. Laughing Kookaburra
18. Common Kingfisher
19. Ruby Throated Hummingbird
20. Toco Toucan
21. Pileated Woodpecker
22. Barn Swallow
23. Cedar Waxwing
24. Eastern Bluebird
25. Brown Thrasher
26. Cardinal
27. American Goldfinch
28. California Quail
29. Common Pheasant
30. Japanese Crane
31. Gray Crowned Crane
32. Barn Owl
33. Belted Kingfisher
34. Red-bellied Woodpecker
35. Purple Martin
36. Scarlet Tanager
37. Red-winged Blackbird
38. House Finch
39. Blue Jay
40. Greater Bird-of-Paradise
41. Hoopoe
42. Goshawk
43. Harlequin Ducks
44. Roadrunner

Name:				
Bird Book Writing				
Student	**1**	**2**	**3**	**Teacher**
	EXAMPLES: Many exciting and realistic examples comparing the birds' parts to other things in the world.	Some examples, comparing the birds' parts to other things in the world.	Very few or not any examples, comparing the birds' parts to other things in the world.	
	DETAIL/ADJECTIVES: Many fancy adjective words that show use of the thesaurus. Very detailed with few common adjectives.	Some adjectives that show use of the thesaurus and give detail.	Use of only common adjectives or not any describing words and provides very little detail.	
	OPENING SENTENCES: Telling what the paragraph is about using some interesting detail or fact about the topic.	Tells us what we'll read about but doesn't give an interesting fact or detail.	A sentence that doesn't tell the reader what they will be reading about.	
	LOGICAL ORDER: All the information that is about the same subtopic is written together before you go on to another subtopic.		The information about the subtopics is mixed up and not written with the other information about the subtopic.	
	TRANSITION SENTENCES: One transition sentence for every new topic paragraph.	Some transition sentences introducing in the paragraph.	No transition sentences as you go from one subtopic to the next in a paragraph.	
	ACTION VERBS: Most verbs used can be found in the thesaurus, and there are very few is or are verbs.	Some action verbs, but a greater use of is or are verbs	Contains mostly is and are as predicates instead of action verbs.	
Total	**Comments**			**Total**

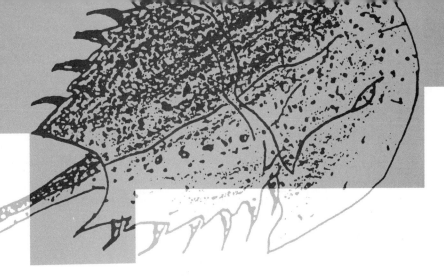

References

Berger, Ron. *A Culture of Quality: A Reflection on Practice.* Providence, R.I.: Annenberg Institute of School Reform, Occasional Paper Series No. 1, 1996.

Brooks, Jacqueline Grennon, and Martin Brooks. *In Search of Understanding: The Case for the Constructivist Classroom.* Alexandria, Va.: ASCD, 1993.

Cousins, Emily, and Melissa Rodgers, eds. *Fieldwork: An Expeditionary Learning Outward Bound Reader.* Dubuque, Iowa: Kendall/Hunt, 1995.

Darling-Hammond, Linda, Jacqueline Ancess, and Beverly Falk. *Authentic Assessment in Action: Studies of Schools and Students at Work.* New York: Teachers College Press, 1995.

Delpit, Lisa. *Other People's Children: Cultural Conflicts in the Classroom.* New York: New Press, 1994.

Duckworth, Eleanor. *The Having of Wonderful Ideas and Other Essays on Teaching and Learning.* New York: Teachers College Press, 1987.

Edwards, Carolyn, Lella Gandini, and George Forman, eds. *The Hundred Languages of Children.* Norwood, N.J.: Ablex, 1993.

Expeditionary Learning Outward Bound Core Practice Benchmarks, Expeditionary Learning Outward Bound, 122 Mount Auburn Street, Cambridge, MA 02138.

Foster, Michele. *Black Teachers on Teaching.* New York: New Press, 1997.

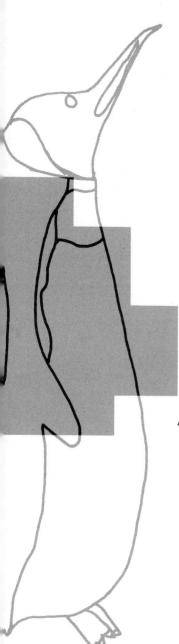

Levy, Steven. *Starting from Scratch: One Classroom Builds Its Own Curriculum.* Portsmouth, N.H.: Heinemann, 1996.

Mednick, Amy, and Emily Cousins, eds. *Fieldwork: An Expeditionary Learning Outward Bound Reader, Volume II.* Dubuque, Iowa: Kendall/Hunt, 1996.

Seidel, Steve, and Joseph Walters, et. al. *Portfolio Practices: Thinking Through the Assessment of Children's Work.* Washington, D.C.: National Education Association School Restructuring Series, 1997.

Steinberg, Adria. *Real Learning, Real Work: School-to-Work as High School Reform.* New York: Routledge, 1998.

Udall, Denis, and Amy Mednick, eds. *Journeys Through Our Classrooms.* Dubuque, Iowa: Kendall/Hunt, 1996.

Wiske, Martha Stone, ed. *Teaching for Understanding: Linking Research with Practice.* San Francisco: Jossey-Bass, 1998.

ADDITIONAL RESOURCES

The National Council of Teachers of English publishes an updated, annotated bibliography series of four booklists covering a wide range of topics. Each booklist is edited by an educator who works with teachers and librarians to review, select, and annotate hundreds of new trade books. The booklists are extensive and practically organized by subject, complete with author, illustrator, subject, and title indexes.

Adventuring with Books: A Booklist for Pre-K–Grade 6, Wendy K. Sutton, ed., and the Committee to Revise the Elementary School Booklist (1997): *Adventuring with Books* contains descriptions of more than 1,200 books published between 1993 and 1995, selected for their high quality and their interest to children ($22.95).

Books for You: An Annotated Booklist for Senior High, Lois T. Staver and Stephanie F. Zenker, eds., and the Committee on the Senior High Booklist (1995): Nearly 1,400 titles, published between 1994 and 1996, are divided into forty thematic groups ($22.95).

Kaleidoscope: A Multicultural Booklist for Grades K-8, Rosalind B. Barrera, Verlinda D. Thompson, and Mark Dressman, eds. (1994): This booklist, focusing on titles that feature people of color, includes nearly 600 annotations. Specific ethnic groups and time periods are identified within the annotations. A list of professional resources for multicultural literature completes the volume ($16. 95).

Your Reading: An Annotated Booklist for Middle School and Junior High, Barbara G. Samuels and G. Kylene Beers, eds. (1996): The book contains more than 1,200 annotations, of which half are on nonfiction subjects from fields like history, the natural and physical sciences, and current events ($21.95).

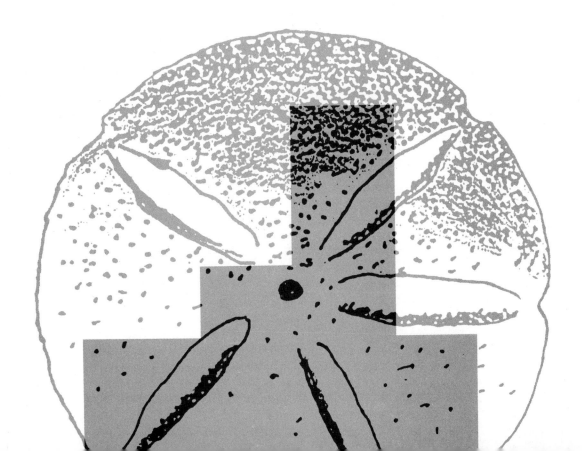

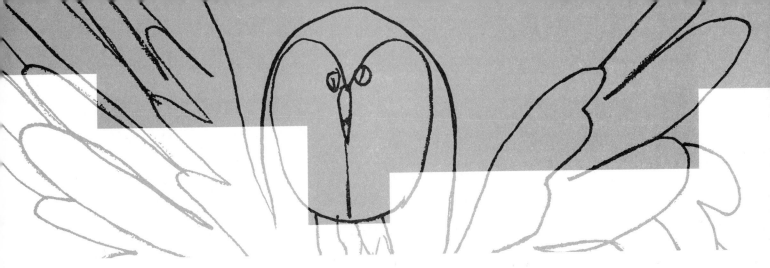

Expeditionary Learning Design Principles[1]

*L*earning is an expedition into the unknown. Expeditions draw together personal experience and intellectual growth to promote self-discovery and the construction of knowledge. We believe that adults should guide students along this journey with care, compassion, and respect for their diverse learning styles, backgrounds, and needs. Addressing individual differences profoundly increases the potential for learning and creativity of each student.

Given fundamental levels of health, safety, and love, all people can and want to learn. We believe Expeditionary Learning harnesses the natural passion to learn and is a powerful method for developing the curiosity, skills, knowledge, and courage needed to imagine a better world and work toward realizing it.

The Primacy of Self-Discovery

Learning happens best with emotion, challenge, and the requisite support. People discover their abilities, values, "grand passions," and responsibilities in situations that offer adventure and the unexpected. They must have tasks that require perseverance, fitness, craftsmanship, imagination, self-discipline, and significant achievement. A primary job of the educator is to help students overcome their fear and discover they have more in them than they think.

The Having of Wonderful Ideas

Teach so as to build on children's curiosity about the world by creating learning situations that provide matter to think about, time to experiment, and time to make sense of what is observed. Foster a community where students' and adults' ideas are respected.

The Responsibility for Learning

Learning is both a personal, individually specific process of discovery and a social activity. Each of us learns within and for ourselves and as a part of a group. Every aspect of a school must encourage children, young people, and adults to become increasingly responsible for directing their own personal and collective learning.

Intimacy and Caring

Learning is fostered best in small groups where there is trust, sustained caring, and mutual respect among all members of the learning community. Keep schools and learning groups small. Be sure there is a caring adult looking after the progress of each child. Arrange for the older students to mentor the younger ones.

Success and Failure

All students must be assured a fair measure of success in learning in order to nurture the confidence and capacity to take risks and rise to increasingly difficult challenges. But it is also important to experience failure, to overcome negative inclinations, to prevail against adversity, and to learn to turn disabilities into opportunities.

Collaboration and Competition

Teach so as to join individual and group development so that the value of friendship, trust, and group endeavor is made manifest. Encourage students to compete, not against each other, but with their own personal best and with rigorous standards of excellence.

Diversity and Inclusivity

Diversity and inclusivity in all groups dramatically increases richness of ideas, creative power, problem-solving ability, and acceptance of others. Encourage students to investigate, value, and draw upon their own different histories, talents, and resources together with those of other communities and cultures. Keep the schools and learning groups heterogeneous.

The Natural World

A direct and respectful relationship with the natural world refreshes the human spirit and reveals the important lessons of recurring cycles and cause and effect. Students learn to become stewards of the earth and of the generations to come.

Solitude and Reflection

Solitude, reflection, and silence replenish our energies and open our minds. Be sure students have time alone to explore their own thoughts, make their own connections, and create their own ideas. Then give them opportunity to exchange their reflections with each other and with adults.

Service and Compassion

We are crew, not passengers, and are strengthened by acts of consequential service to others. One of a school's primary functions is to prepare its students with the attitudes and skills to learn from and be of service to others.

---

[1] The above principles have been informed by Kurt Hahn's "Seven Laws of Salem," by Paul Ylvisaker's "The Missing Dimension," and by Eleanor Duckworth's *"The Having of Wonderful Ideas" and Other Essays on Teaching and Learning* (New York: Teachers College Press, 1987).

Outward Bound USA
100 Mystery Point Rd.
Garrison, NY 10524-9757
(914) 424-4000

Expeditionary Learning Outward Bound
122 Mount Auburn St.
Cambridge, MA 02138
(617) 576-1260
info@elob.org
http://www.elob.org